George Duckworth Atkin

House scraps

George Duckworth Atkin

House scraps

ISBN/EAN: 9783337152444

Printed in Europe, USA, Canada, Australia, Japan

Cover: Foto ©Andreas Hilbeck / pixelio.de

More available books at **www.hansebooks.com**

THE MILLENNIUM; OR, THE UNION OF CHRISTENDOM.

[FOR PRIVATE CIRCULATION ONLY.]

HOUSE SCRAPS

Collected by
G. Duckworth Atkin

With illustrations by
Geo. Cruickshank.
F C Gould
Lucien Davis &c.

"Laugh, and be well. Monkeys have been
Extreme good Doctors for the Spleen ;
And Kittens, if the humour hit,
Have harlequined away the Fit."

"The Spleen"
Matthew Green.

Entered at Gorgonzola Hall.
Published by the Author at the Stock Exchange
LONDON. 1887

[ENTERED AT STATIONERS' HALL.]

To

WILLIAM CHAMBERLAIN,

his Oldest and Most Respected Stock Exchange Friend,

this Book is dedicated by

THE COMPILER.

PREFACE.

THE compiler of this collection of Stock Exchange *facetiæ* trusts that his hope of its being enjoyed and appreciated by his fellow Members may, at least for their own sakes, prove to be realised. It has been his humble endeavour to make it include all the stories, anecdotes, incidents, jokes, gibes, retorts,

"Jests, and youthful jollities,
Quips, and cranks, and wanton wiles,"

which, from time to time, have amused the House, or "set it in a roar." Great care has been observed, he hopes with success, to exclude anything in any way calculated to cause offence or annoyance, the personages of every tale, or practical joke, being veiled in anonymity.

He thanks Mr. F. C. GOULD and Mr. J. J. RAMSAY for their kind assistance. The extracts from *Punch* are included, by the kind permission of its proprietors. He has also to thank the proprietors of the "*Stock Exchange*" for allowing him to reproduce the sketch of the Stock Exchange in May, 1887, one of the welcome productions of the pliant pencil of Mr. F. C. GOULD.

Like other *arcana*, those of the Stock Exchange have been pretty generally revealed. It is well enough known that nowhere else is there a keener enjoyment felt for wit and humour than by its Members. If any remain who are likely to think this paradoxical, and wonder how it can be that men are not too much engrossed there, in money making, to find the time for making or appreciating jokes, let them call to mind how very close together always lie the fountains of laughter and tears. The gravest pursuits are not merely compatible with, but predispose the mind even for, simple enjoyment. Both jobbers and brokers will own that their minds have often been cheered, and their energies vivified, by one or other of many of the "Happy Thoughts" collected in this little volume. May it be permitted to become their *vade mecum!* When the former are hard-up for "turns," they can try a turn of it, and if Commissions run short at times, for the latter, they, too, might derive consolation from its pages, for there is the warrant of Horace for it, that—

Dulce est desipere in lo(w) *co*(mos).

STOCK EXCHANGE,
    December, 1887.

HOUSE SCRAPS.

The following is a copy of a printed piece of paper, found with some other documents in the box of a very old member of the Stock Exchange. Half the paper is missing, and there is nothing to denote at what period it was printed :—

2 Pilgrims Gowen with a Noble Marter and a Crosse.
A Hoare with a Tucker (Pryce a Penny), a Sly Hussey with Love and a Lear, and a Bilke, a Coward, and a Bully.
Two Andrews and a Norman Chevallier May by Chance Chant a Carrol and a Medley.
A Sherriff with Law, 3 Baileys and 2 Duns.
A Cook with a Leak and a Bone, and a Crisp Fry with Pickles.
A Collier with Cole. Three Turners with Wood and 2 Bannisters.
Two Barbers with Combes Curling a Platt. A Taylor with Corderoy. A Miller with Mills.
A Smith with a Keane Axe, a Ward and Staples, and 2 Smiths with Stubbs, a Flint, a Steel and Sparkes, 2 Bells and a Pulley.
A Mason with a Heap, and a Goldsmith with Gould, Pearse a Seton with Aickin Fayne.
Two Packers with Cotton Webb, and a Shearer with a Tod.
A Gardener with a Garland and Flowers, a Rose with 2 Budds, a Bee, 2 Vines, and a Plant with a Cherry and 2 Peppercorns.
A Dyer with two Greens, 4 Browns, White, and 2 Greys.
A Town with 3 Halls, 3 Streets, and 2 Wells by Townsend.
A Cape with Fields, a Brooke with a Fall, a Vale and 2 Hills with a Rutt and 2 Ridges, Groves, Woods, Birch, Fearn, Underwood, Greenwoods, a Woodhouse and Barnes.

*** The House of Call for Wheelers, Coopers, a Plummer and Painter, a Baker, a Tanner, a Thatcher, a Porter, a Butler, a Slater, and a Potter.

Messages and Letters conveyed by the Porter by a simple Method (quicker than by the Telegraph) to
Dover, Lancaster, Hull, Sheffield, Berkley, Abington, Wakefield, and Ross.
Some few Names are spelled according to their Pronunciation.

EVANS AND RUFFY, Printers, 29, Budge Row, Wallbrook.

A TIP.

A. " I say, old man! do you want to make some money? "
B. " Rather. I'm on."
A. " Well, go and buy yourself ten Unified." (*They part.*)

A few days later, when they meet again, the stock having meanwhile fallen 2 or 3 per cent., the conversation takes the following turn :—

A. " I am awfully sorry about the tip I gave you the other day."
B. " Don't name it, my dear fellow. Why, when *you* told me to *buy* myself ten, I immediately went and *sold* ten, and have just bought them back at 2 per cent. profit."

There is a certain coolness between the parties now.

SCENE.—*Washing-room in the Old House.**

Member (noted for using two or three basins when washing). " I say, waiter, I suppose we shall have plenty of accommodation in the new washing-room?"

Waiter. "Yes, sir; but I do not think there will be a swimming-bath attached to it."

* The accommodation in the old washing-room was very limited; the basins were fitted with miserable little taps, and when turned on full it generally took about a minute to fill a basin and another minute for the water to run away.

AN EXPENSIVE WALL-PAPER.

A young man once called upon the directors of a certain mining company, and asked them to come round and inspect a room in his house. The father of the young man owned a quantity of shares in this company, and it seeming not at all likely that the mine would ever do any good, he had used them to paper the walls of this room. Some gold was afterwards found in the mine, so that the shares at once became of considerable value. The directors admitted the bonds on the walls were genuine, but how to get them off was the problem which seemed insoluble. Pulling the house down was suggested by some, while others advised using steam. I believe the directors ultimately issued new shares, and had the others torn down.

A NEW USE FOR BONDS.

It is extraordinary how careless some people are with their bonds and certificates. The following facts, which came under my notice in 1886, afford an astonishing case in point. An old lady, living in a primitive provincial town, held a quantity of Dutch Bonds to bearer. About the year 1857 she used several of them as a covering for jam pots, trimming the edges freely with a pair of scissors. She took due care, it seems, of the rest of the bonds, and sent in the talons every seven or eight years for a fresh supply of coupons, the dividends being regularly paid up to 1886. In 1882, the lady dying, the bonds came into the possession of some relations, when all the very peculiar facts of the case came out. When the bonds had to be sent in for conversion in 1886, several people were able to identify the handwriting on them—"Strawberry Jam, 1st Lot, 1857,"—as that of the deceased, whilst the marks of the rim of the jam pots, which were plainly visible on the bonds, conclusively proved in what a singular fashion she had seen fit to *preserve* them.

A parallel to this odd case appears in the act of another lady, who, finding her bonds were printed on stiff paper, used them to "back up" a quilt with. The Government has continued to pay the coupons, but insisted upon having the quilt in its possession.

Another old gentleman used to wrap his bonds up in a large sheet of brown paper, and when he died the brown paper was found wrapped up in the bonds.

INDECISION!

An old lady, who had £1,500 left her, got the money in bank notes, which she kept twenty-six years before she could make up her mind what to invest it in.

"Fifty shares at $\frac{1}{16}$, Mr. D——?"

"No; I am afraid I can't deal with you at $1\frac{1}{8}$, but I will make you $\frac{7}{8}-\frac{7}{8}$ in them."

"All right, I shall sell you fifty."

I once saw a transfer upon which the witness had written the following:—

Name.—Henry Johnstone.
Address.—Ivy Cottage, Pembroke.
Description.—5 feet 9 inches, fair, blue eyes.

A West-End swell was once introduced to the House as the authorised clerk of one of the best firms of brokers in the Stock Exchange. He was not a very brilliant youth, and when he walked into the Consol market and asked the price, and was told "seven, nine" ($\frac{7}{16}$, $\frac{9}{16}$), he laughed very loudly and said, "Go on! don't think I'm going to be taken in like that, make me a ¼ price and I'll deal with you."

A CURIOUS MISTAKE.

The following story is told of a very old member, who enjoyed his wine, and always took great care of it when he happened to pick up a choice parcel. Many years ago, when he was living in a fashionable street in the West-End, he chanced to buy a large cask of very fine old port, which he had placed at the extreme end of his cellar; and to make perfectly sure that it should not be touched, he had a wall built across the cellar, and so closed it in. A year or two after this, when he was dining with one of his neighbours, some fine port was placed upon the table after dinner. Several glasses having been drunk, our member asked where he could get some port like it. "Well, old fellow, I will let you into a secret, but don't say anything about it. I was having some alterations made in my cellar lately, when we discovered that some old fool who lived in this house before me had built a wall round a large cask of port, and had forgotten all about it, and this is some of it, and I am afraid there isn't much left." The effect upon our worthy member's feelings may be better imagined than described.

A concert was once advertised all over the House, to be given by the Stock Exchange Orchestral Society. On the eve of the concert, a jocular jobber was chaffing one of the committee of the society, and said he knew there were any number of tickets knocking about, and that they were at a discount. "That's all you know about it; what price will you make me in five 7s. 6d. tickets?" said the committeeman. "I'll make you five to six shillings in five." "All right, old man, I shall *sell* you five." And what is more, he had to take them.

Two piscatorial members were talking over family affairs, and one informed the other that he had lately become the father of a most interesting little baby. "And how big is it?" asked his friend.

"Oh, I don't exactly know; say about as big as a *twelve-pound cod*."

A Double Option.

A KNOWING CORPSE.

One afternoon, when the dividend on a certain bank stock was expected to be announced every moment, a broker went into the market and wanted to deal in fifty shares. "My dear fellow," said the jobber, "we expect the dividend every minute, and I really can't make you a price." The broker seemed very much put out, murmured something about wanting to settle up a deceased account, and as he had a long list of stocks in his hand, the dealer thinking he was certain to be a seller, made him a price, and he (the broker) bought them. Soon afterwards the dividend was announced, and the shares at once rose about £2. The next time our jobber saw his friend, he said, "I say, old man, don't you think that was rather a knowing old corpse of yours?"

A LIBERAL MEMBER.

It was the custom of a very old member, whose liberal instincts were not very marked, to take all his securities home with him in a hackney coach. One evening he left his bags in the cab, which at once drove away. He went to his dinner, and soon after the butler coming in to say that "cabby" had brought back his bags, he told his servant to give the man a *shilling*, and quietly continued his meal.

H—— B—— happened to be a large bull of a certain stock and the market went very much against him. Feeling somewhat savage, he told his friend C—— K—— that he wished the whole place was in flames. K—— quietly remarked, "I should have thought it was hot enough for you already, old fellow!"

GOING BETTER.

One afternoon our leading salvationist walked into the Mexican Railway market, and said in deep tones "Have you heard that the General has purchased all our sins?"

Rude Member: "No! Has he really; does he think they are going better?"

AN HEIR AND SON.

When the Queen of Spain gave birth to a son in May, 1886, the following notice was posted in the Spanish market:—

"In consequence of the birth of a King of Spain the Spanish market now rejoices in its *Aronson* (heir and son)."

Mr. Aronson was a jobber in the market.

United Mex. doth me perplex,
Mysore is quite as bad,
The Potosi doth worry me,
But Del Rey drives me mad.

A PLEASANT SURPRISE.

A mining company once had recourse to a clever trick in order to make a call on its shares. They were nominally of £1 each, 17s. paid, and were "scrip to bearer." One day the directors astonished their shareholders by declaring a dividend of 8d. per share; the shares had to be deposited at the company's office to be marked. When nearly all the shares had been deposited, and the names and addresses of the holders had been obtained, the directors quietly made a call of 3s. per share, much to the disgust of the unfortunate holders.

It was at the Annual Dinner of the Benevolent Fund, some years ago, when a prominent member rose and said, "I hope the success of the Fund will be as great in the *past* as it has been in the *future*."

A young member, who was not very particular what became of his H's, was presented by his wife with a blooming boy. The next morning a piece of paper was stuck on his back with the following written across it:—"The wife of 'Enery B——, of 'Averstock 'Ill, of a Sun and Air."

HOUSE SCRAPS.

A lady recently wrote to her broker to acknowledge the receipt of some bonds, and told him that she had "torn up the *advertisement part*, and taken great care of the *little bits you cut off.*"

A member who used to live on the banks of the Thames was once heard grumbling about the continual downpour of rain, which had caused floods all over the country; he said, "formerly the *river* was at the *bottom* of my *garden*, but now my *garden* is at the *bottom* of the *river.*"

A broker once invested about £190, for an old lady, in a company which was considered very safe and steady. For six years she received a cheque for £8. 12s. per annum as dividend, but during the late depression in trade the company earned a smaller dividend, and she only received a cheque for £6. 13s. She at once wrote to her broker and told him that she could "put up with a lot of things," but she wasn't going "to be done out of her proper dividend; I really cannot do without it;" and she finished up by asking him "to call at the company's office and get the cheque altered."

Fragment of "Hymn to St. Chittles," as chanted by the members of the House, A.D. 1583.

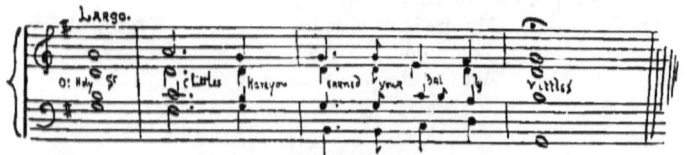

At the time of the breaking out of the Russian War, in 1853, old Sam Chard went into the Consol market and enquired if there was anything doing. "Well, there is nothing much doing; but I hear the Russians have taken umbrage———." "The deuce they have," says Chard; and he at once rushed away and told everybody that the Russians had captured Umbrage. About two hours later he walked up to his friend and said, "I say, where the devil is Umbrage; I can't find it on the map?"

SYDNEY SMITH ON CONSOLS.

The warlike power of every country depends on its Three per Cents. If Cæsar were to reappear on earth, Wetenhall's list would be more important than his Commentaries; Rothschild would open and shut the Temple of Janus; Thomas Baring or Bates would probably command the Tenth Legion, and the soldiers would march to battle with loud cries of "Scrip and Omnium Reduced! Consols and Cæsar!"

Rev. Sydney Smith.

Two friendly jobbers, once upon a time, sat talking on a seat in the Consol market. Said one, "I should like to sell five consols at $\frac{3}{8}$, wouldn't you?"

"Yes, I should."

"Then I'll *buy* five of you."

The north wind doth blow and we shall have snow,
And what will the bulls do then, poor things;
Unprepared for the shock, they will sell all their stock,
And the bears will get hold of the tin, poor things."

Some years ago, when Mexican were about 56, a broker went into the market and asked the price. "I'll make you $\frac{3}{4}$—6 in five, sir."

"I shall sell you five."

"Look here, sir, I'll give you $\frac{5}{8}$ for your *balance*."

"Then I sell you *ninety-five thousand*," quietly said the broker.

A certain German gentleman, not a hundred miles from the Spanish market, got cross one day with some members who were teasing him, and informed them that "*familiarity breeds contemptuosity.*"

Two or three members sat talking in the Consol market, when a jobber from another part of the House passing by, one member said, "I say, William, who's that man with the light bags?"

"Confound it! I've forgotten his name for the moment, but he's *with Child.*"

"Good gracious! you don't say so; why, I never heard of such a thing."

When Sir J. Parsons and Mr. Shirreff were directors of the Metropolitan Railway, about 1867, the stock fell very rapidly in price, and numerous letters appeared in the papers, warning people against investing in it.

The following lines were posted in the House:—

"Why need we these letters of warning? we dealers in bargains Metrop,
With *Parsons* and *Shirreff* directors, of course we prepare for the *drop!*"

A broker once asked for a price in 20,000 Trunks, when the market was in a very excited state, and the price was not the same for ten seconds at a time; the jobber made him $\frac{1}{4}$—$\frac{3}{8}$, but he wanted a closer price, and the jobber in a rather irritated manner, said: "Shew me your 'wire' and I'll make you a $\frac{1}{16}$ price." The broker quietly handed him the telegram, which read:—"Close my twenty Trunks at best."

COOL!

It was on the occasion of some great meeting at the Mansion House that one of our members made himself famous (for a short time). As he was passing, he observed a great crowd round the building, and, being curious to know what was going on, he walked up to the principal door, but seeing he had no chance of getting in there, he went round to the Lord Mayor's private entrance, and was passing in when a policeman stopped him and said, "You can't come in here, sir." Our member, who was only about 5 ft. 3 in. in his boots, stared at him in a most contemptuous manner and said in very indignant tones, "Do you know who I am, sir!" The policeman, taken by surprise, and thinking he had made a mess of it, touched his helmet, and meekly said, "Oh! I beg your pardon sir, I really did not recognise you for the moment," and allowed him to pass on.

Vocal and Instrumental.

A member having heard the above story, determined to try the same dodge upon the first opportunity, and soon afterwards, being in the neighbourhood of the Houses of Parliament, attempted to enter by the member's door, but a policeman stopped him. Drawing himself up and glaring savagely at the "bobby," he said, "Do you know who I am, sir!" "No" answered the policeman, "and what's more I don't want to, just clear out of this or I'll run yer in." He cleared.

The following lines were written about the Stock Exchange Orchestral Society during 1885, after a concert given in aid of the Clerks' Provident Fund, when a profit of about £60 was made. I have only copied a few extracts relating to the members. The concert was a great success.

THE STOCK EXCHANGE ORCHESTRAL SOCIETY.

Those trumpet blasts! their echoes tell,
The notes of ancient *Vandervell*,
With *Harris*, while the silv'ry bray
Of the euphonium borne by *Gray*
Rings out upon the silent air,
With *Riches* bass and *Delamare*.

* * * *

And *Kitchin's* style is simply grand,
He wields his bow with skilful hand.
Out *Vandervell* and *Robertson*,
Your echoes *Pallant* thunder on.

* * * *

Why stands apart and holds aloof
In moody silence *Pelham Rooff*?
When Santley pales to hear his name,
Who festive Reeves puts down to shame,
Oh break my harp her choicest string,
Why was not *Pelham* asked to sing?

* * * *

Kind muse, descend thy voice to raise
The conduct of our *Kitchin* praise,
  Who led our bows to victory.
Sternberg, with gallant *Halberstadt*,
Brown, *Bower*, and *Gardner*, one and all,
With *Coldwells* of the Erie crew.
Higgins and *Lewin*, *Lovey*, *Pawle*,
Whose strains profound might well recall
The fair of Saint *Bartholomew*
  Before its valedictory.
As loud as clarion sounds for war,
Rings out the well-deserved encore,
Well earned! that oft repeated call
That night in old Saint *Andrew's* hall;
Atkin, and second fiddlers all,
I watch'd thine elbows rise and fall;
Nor failed to mark and note full well,
Fatt, *Crosdale*, and *Hurst Daniell*.
With *Gray* and *Cork*, and *Cooke* to boot,
And *Battiscombe* to follow suit.
Well might the first be famed for dash,
He fingers both the bow and cash.
Now pause we here to make appeal
To aid our good librarian—*Veall*

HOUSE SCRAPS.

The man who sorts and fixes
The manuscripts of all his friends,
The music, books, and odds and ends;
      Which (by the way) he mixes!
An octave of great 'cellos played
Like demons for a wager laid;
Assisted by violas seven,
The fallen angels of this heaven.
They might have played to old King *Cole*,
They played so well upon the whole;
While *Falconer* and *Whitefield* plied
Their oboes till spectators cried;
And *Wildy's* notes from silvery flute
Recalled the famed arcadian lute;
Till down came thunders of applause,
From all the men who make our laws,
Our Stock Exchange nobility!
Mid smiles of many a lady fair,
L.—— Baker wriggled in his chair,
While *Charlesworth* hugged both *Lobb* and *Wedd*,
With bursting mirth he faintly said
      Away with grief and sorrow.
Great *Edwin Lawrence* seized the hat,
He brushes up so smooth and flat,
While *Chinnery* his kerchief plied,
And *Chamberlain* exulting cried
      I'd come again to-morrow.

J. F. H. R., THE PRESIDENT OF THE GREAT S. E. O. S.

A LIST OF SLANG WORDS IN COMMON USE IN THE HOUSE, WITH THEIR MEANINGS.

A Rumpty, or a Tooth	A $\frac{1}{32}$ part of £1.
A Fiddle	A $\frac{1}{16}$ part of £1.
Jam Tart	Exactly the market. Buyers and sellers at the same price.
A Turn	The profit on a bargain.
A Rasper	A big "turn."
A Kidney	A corruption of a man's name, "Cadney," who is first known to have dealt under $\frac{1}{32}$. A fractional part of 1s.
A Picker-up	A man who tries to get members to make a wrong price, and then deals with them.
A Back-handed Turn	Having made an unprofitable bargain.
To Bang	To loudly offer stock with the intention of lowering the price.
To Puff	To loudly bid for stock with the intention of sending up the price.
A Bull	A man who buys stock in hopes of a rise.
A Stale Bull	A man who has held stock for a long period without profit.
A Bear	A man who has sold stock which he does not possess in hopes of buying it back again at a profit.
A Stale Bear	A man who has sold stock which he does not possess, and has not bought it back. A bear who has been short of stock for a considerable period.
A Stag	A man who applies for shares or stock in a new company with the intention of selling as soon as possible at a premium.
A Lame Duck	A defaulter.
A Squirt	A man who hangs about a market with a paltry order, and who will not deal fairly.
A Tape-worm	A man who walks about the House collecting prices of different stocks to telegraph on the "Tape."
A Wire-worm	A man who collects prices to "wire" to country clients.
An Orchid	A member with a "handle" to his name.
A Shunter	A man who buys or sells stocks on the chance of undoing his business, on one of the provincial Stock Exchanges, at a profit.
To Hammer	To declare a man a defaulter.
To Corner	To get the entire control of a stock and so make it impossible for a man to complete his bargains.
To Read	To try to tell by a man's face or manner what he wants to do.
To Shoot	To make a man a close price in a stock without knowing if there would be a profit or loss on the bargain.
Gorgonzola Hall	The nick-name for the Stock Exchange, so named on account of the marble walls.

Cutting his own Throat	To buy or sell stocks, and immediately re-sell or re-purchase them at a loss.
Opening his Mouth too Wide	Getting excited and bidding for large amounts of stock, and getting "landed" with it.
All in!	An expression used when a market goes flat and there is a general disposition to sell.
All out!	An expression used when a market goes better and there is a general disposition to buy.
Buy a Prop!	A term used when a market is flat and there is nobody to support it.
Fourteen Hundred!	A pass-word used when a stranger is seen in the House.
A Runner	A man attached to a broker's office, who, having a private connection, employs his time in running from client to client in search of orders.
Bucket Shop	The office of an outside broker of doubtful character.
A Sweater	A broker who cuts down commissions. A broker who works for such small commissions as to prevent other brokers getting the business, whilst hardly being profitable to himself.
A Poacher	A jobber who deals out of his own market. Also applied to a jobber who is continually changing his market.
To Rig	To unduly inflate a security by fair means or foul.
Spread, Straddle	Americanisms for "Options."

When the first addition was made to the House in 1853, the screen which separated the old House from the new was pulled down before the alterations were completed, and as the building looked very bare, a large mirror was placed over the New Court entrance in a recess corresponding to the windows in the American market; owing to a defect in the mirror, or the manner in which it was mounted, it caused the roof of the new part of the building to appear altogether out of the level, giving rise to much amusement and the following lines:—

> "When first unveil'd, what wonder met our view
> In our new House, from cavil Envy shrunk;
> But see what work a glass too much can do,
> And ask, is Cole, the House, or am I drunk?"

"Lord Ernest Hamilton is retiring from the Army in order to become a member of the Stock Exchange."—*Truth*.

> A Paradox this seems to be,
> Whereat some folks may mock,
> A soldier for the Stock Exchange
> Must now exchange his Stock.
> From *Punch*, 19/1/'84.

"AN ORCHID IN A TURNIP FIELD."

A young sprig of nobility, who was admitted to the House as the unauthorised clerk of a dealer in the American market, was once heard to tell a friend that when he was in the House he felt like "an *orchid in a turnip field.*" It is almost needless to say that he very shortly had cause to regret his speech, as ever afterwards he and his friends were known as "orchids," and what with the chaff from some members, and the snubbing he got from others, he was very glad to leave the House. By degrees "an orchid" has become the nick-name for any member with a "handle" to his name.

THE DONKEY'S LAMENT.

On the 26th August, 1856, Mr. George Hoy, of 7, Chester Street, Green Street, Bethnal Green, sent a challenge to the directors of the Eastern Counties Railway, to run his donkey against some of their business trains. He has since run against and beaten them. The following lines were written on the occasion and posted in the House, and called the "Donkey's Lament."

> "Who'd ever have thought, I should live to be brought
>   To so grievous and sad a disaster,
> As thus to be backed 'gainst this railway so crack'd,
>   Just as if I couldn't do it no faster.
>
> I wouldn't a minded how hard I'd a grinded
>   To run the Great Northern or Western ;
> But only to go 'gainst this slow-going Co.!
>   Is a thing as don't suit my digestion.
>
> I know I can beat 'em or else I will eat 'em,
>   But wants to do summat worth doing,
> Kos any poor Ass these 'ere Easterns can pass,
>   So there won't be no credit ensuing.
>
> I wishes my Master had spared this disaster
>   To me, his poor faithful old slave ;
> But as he has done it, of course I shall run it,
>   And Victory be to the Brave.

STOCK EXCHANGE IDIOMS, 1850—1886.

Here he is!!!
Buy! buy!
You'll have enough of 'em!
I've seen 'em look better!
Done at $\frac{5}{8}$, the rubbish!
You've all got 'em!
Let me out! let me out!
T. O. P!
Have you seen my Tommy?
Buy one at a larry-cum-do.
Getting gravelly here!
Done at $\frac{7}{8}$, knowing hands slipping 'em!
Done at $\frac{3}{4}$, bringing 'em in!
Here they are quietly good!
You may have a pony at the 15!
I look to the Bank!
Sell one at a fiddle!
Up or down, you have 'em!
I'll have a shy, if I lose my stick!
I'm in! I'm in!!
Buy one at a rum-cum-bum!
Show us your motive!
At $\frac{3}{4}$ you may help yourselves!
Done at $\frac{5}{8}$ a whole-un!
R——y!!!
They're getting toosey-moosey!
You're all out!!
Hold 'em up!!!
Done at a rumpty; cards picking 'em up!
Buy one for the protracted period!
Sell two for the long trot!
Call o'more all your life!
That's a long ride!
P. and C. for the coming event!
Another armistice!!
Bradock's hat!!!
Let 'em down gently!!
Buy a prop!!

Done at a fiddle; "Sugar" getting in!!
I'm nothing but a buyer!!
Any volume, my pippin?
Ecod, in a month they'll be unsaleable!!
Any cove got a book?
Sell! sell! you're all in a mess!!
Quare! quare!
Dead Horse! Dead Horse!
Mind your pockets!
I'll go and see my man.
Sell one at a Cadney!
Another row!!
Two more men don't speak!!
All in the cart!!
Fourteen hundred!!
Give us a bit!
Oranges! oranges!
So I'll take five!
It's all done to stop the rise!
They've knocked the bottom out of 'em.
At $\frac{5}{8}$ for next go, lay 'em in.
At $\frac{3}{4}$, let go the painter!
Done at $\frac{1}{4}$, a monkey!
Who got the turn?
Done at the 11; pulling for 'em.
Buy five at $\frac{1}{16}$ for the deferential!
Very well; you're looking!
What are you laughing at?
Who bought the rabbit?
It's all settled!!!
Another wine party!!
He has taken a front seat.
Ninety won't stop 'em!!
Got a turn to chuck away?
Give five away!!
Another panic.
Sawdust!! sawdust!!

LIST OF NICK-NAMES OF STOCK EXCHANGE SECURITIES

ABBREVIATIONS OMITTED.

Ales	Allsopp & Sons Ord. Stk.
Apes	Atlantic 1st Mortgage Bonds.
Ayrshires	Glasgow & South-Western Rly. Ord. Stk.
Bags	Buenos Ayres Great Southern Rly. Ord. Stk.
Beetles	Colorado United Mining Co. Shares.
Berthas	London, Brighton & South Coast Rly. Def. Ord. Stk.
Berwicks	North-Eastern Rly. Consolidated Ord. Stk.
Bones	Wickens, Pease & Co. Shares.
Bottles	Barrett's Brewery & Bottling Co.
Brums	London & North-Western Rly. Ord. Stk.
Bulgarian Atrocities	Varna & Rustchuk Rly. 3 per cent. Obligations.
Caleys	Caledonian Rly. Ord. Stk.
Claras	Caledonian Rly. Def. Ord. Stk.
Chats	London, Chatham & Dover Rly.
Chinas	Eastern Extension Telegraph Shares.
Cohens	Turks, 1869. (Now Group III.)
Cottons	Confederate Dollar Bonds.
Cream-jugs	Charkof-Krementschug Rly. Bonds.
Dinahs	Edinburgh & Glasgow Rly. Ord. Stk.
Dogs	Newfoundland Land Co. Shs.
Doras	South-Eastern Rly. Def. Ord. Stk.
Dovers	South-Eastern Rly. Ord. Stk.
Ducks	Aylesbury Dairy Co. Shs.
Haddocks	Great North of Scotland Ord. Stk.
Kisses	Hotchkiss Ordnance Co. Shs.
Knackers	Harrison, Barber & Co. Shs.
Leeds	Lancashire & Yorkshire Rly. Ord. Stk.
Mails	Mexican Rly. Ord. Stk.
Megs	Mexican Rly. 1st Preference Stock.
Matches	Bryant & May Shs.
Mets	Metropolitan Rly. Ord. Stk.
Middies	Midland Rly. Ord. Stk.
Muttons	Turks, 1873. (Now in Group III.)
Noras	Great Northern Rly. Def. Ord. Stk.
Nuts	Barcelona Tramway Shs.
Pots	North Staffordshire Rly. Ord. Stk.
Pigtails	Chartered Bank of India, Australia & China.
Roses	Buenos Ayres & Rosario Rly. Ord. Stk.
Rollers	United States Rolling Stock.
Sarahs	Manchester, Sheffield & Lincolnshire Rly. Def. Stk.
Sardines	Royal Sardinian Rly. Shs.
Shores	Lake Shore & Michigan Southern Rly. Shs.

Sarah's Boots .	Sierra Buttes Gold Mine Shs.
Silvers . . .	India Rubber, Gutta Percha & Telegraph Works Co. Shs.
Souths . . .	London & South-Western Rly. Ord. Stk.
Stouts . . .	Arthur Guinness, Son & Co. Shares.
Sunshades . .	{ Sunchales Extension of the Buenos Ayres & Rosario Rly. Co. Shs.
Vestas . . .	Railway Investment Co. Def. Stk.
Virgins . . .	Virginia New Funded.
Whip-sticks .	Dunaberg & Witepsk Rly. Shs.
Yorks . . .	Great Northern Rly. Ord. Stk.

Sheik-el-Himing

A previous Secretary of the Stock Exchange was very much at sea in his grammar. A story goes that the committee, hearing that a collection had been made for the 5th November to provide a grand display of fireworks, asked the Secretary to issue a notice to stop it. One was accordingly issued, but in so illiterate a style that the next day the following verse was put up in the House:—

> " The money who collected were
> For fireworks intended,
> Shall in the purchase of a Lind-
> Ley Murray be expended.
> Because the members of the ' 'Ouse '
> Considers it a pity,
> To see such 'orrid grammar used
> By Managers and Committee."

A CLASSIFIED LIST OF THE MEMBERS OF THE STOCK EXCHANGE, 1862.

1 Abbey	3 Fields	2 Kings	6 Whites	6 Prices
2 Monks	5 Woods	2 Knights	7 Brownes	and
1 Palmer	2 Fenns	1 Marshall	4 Grays	1 Stock.
1 Crosse	1 Heath	1 Chamberlain	and	
and	1 Foard	and	1 Green.	3 Walkers
1 Idle.	1 Frith	1 Major.	———	and
———	7 Hills	———	1 Kitchen	1 Trotter.
2 Chappells	2 Peakes	1 Bigg	1 Cook	———
2 Bishops	3 Ridges	1 Little	and	1 Love
1 Deacon	3 Wells	1 Small	2 Frys.	1 Vertue
3 Chaplins	1 Flower	1 Short	———	and
2 Parsons	2 Peppercornes	and	1 Lowe	1 Grace.
and	and	1 Tootall.	1 Vile	———
2 Clarkes.	2 Capers.	———	and	1 Case
———	1 Badger	1 Whitehead	1 Towgood.	and
	1 Bullock	and	———	1 Key.
1 Baker	1 Fox	2 Woolleys.	2 Upwards	———
6 Barbers	1 Wolfe	———	and	1 Smart
1 Butcher	3 Lyons	1 Shepherd	2 Downers.	and
2 Skinners	1 Drake	and	———	2 Paines.
13 Smiths	1 Goose	1 Crook.	1 North	———
1 Chandler	1 Peacock	———	and	1 Foote
4 Coopers	2 Starlings	2 Barnes	2 Wests.	and
3 Turners	3 Worms	1 Hall	———	1 Nutt.
1 Cheeseman	and	1 Lodge	1 Bone	———
4 Taylors	1 Crabb.	and	and	1 "Spider"
1 Pittman	———	1 Backhouse.	2 Smallbones.	and
1 Tyler	1 Ball	———	———	2 Webbs.
1 Mason	2 Bells	2 Vignes	1 Sturdy	———
1 Porter	2 Blocks	1 Thorne	1 Hardy	1 Stewart
1 Butler	4 Pulleys	1 Ferne	1 Haggard	and
1 Gardner	1 Waite	and	and	2 Tudors.
1 Faulconer	1 Cleaver	1 Bush.	1 Hale.	———
1 Hunter	2 Cannons	———	———	And in all
and	4 Carrs	1 Blunt	1 Rigg	1 Sex.
1 Forester.	1 Cork	1 Keen	and	
	and	and	2 Bilkes	
	1 Pott.	1 Sharpe.		

The following appeared in the *Financial News*, in January, 1885:—

THE NEW STOCK EXCHANGE BUILDING.

"The members of the Stock Exchange will take possession of their new building to-day. The ceremonies will be very simple but impressive; and we have been favoured with the following programme, which has been adopted for the occasion. After the customary opening prayer in the foreign market, the members will join in singing the inaugural hymn, "I dreamt I dwelt in marble halls," the solo being rendered by a well-known member in the Trunk market. The opening address will then be delivered by Mr. John Prust, who will turn the building over to the committee, which is considered a very good 'turn.' A procession will then be formed in the following order:—

THE COMMITTEE.
Mr. Lawrence Baker.
The Blue Ribbon Army and the Brothers Reid.
The Decayed Members.
Messrs. John A. Garle and Gus Wildy.
The Widows and Orphans, headed by Mr. Waller.
Mr. Streeten cum Circular.
Messrs. Cawston, Charlesworth & Co., carrying Turks.
Mr. W. R. Hartridge, carrying a begrudged ninepence.
Members <i>en masse</i>.
Members on foot.
Mr. Thwaites."

The proceedings will close with a performance of the Turkish *réveille* on a Jew's harp, and, after a walk round, there will be a distribution of Gorgonzola cheese and Pyemont's port at the expense of the proprietors of the Stock Exchange.

One afternoon when the markets were dull all over the House, and things were very unsettled, a knowing broker walked into the Spanish market and asked Murray Richardson the price. Murray tried to "read" him, and then said:—

"They are $\frac{3}{8}-\frac{1}{2}$, sir,"

"I sell you ten."

"Excuse me, sir, I was about to observe, when you so *rudely interrupted* me, that although they call them $\frac{3}{8}-\frac{1}{2}$, *I'm* not a *buyer*."

NOT TO BE CAUGHT.

When the new building was nearly finished the managers engaged several new waiters. These poor fellows had plenty to do to get accustomed to the working arrangements. When one of them was placed at one of the doors to call the members from the inside, somebody asked him to call "Hokey! Pokey!" and such like names, until he called a prominent member by his nick-name, when there was a row, and he was told he would be reported. The next day when he was asked to call "Partridge Greenfield!" he said, "No thank you, sir, they *had* me yesterday."

OVER PAR.

A certain highly-respectable member—all highly-respectable men have large families—having just had an addition made to his family of seven—four boys and three girls—his fellow members hailed him, as soon as they got wind of it, as "par to an eighth."

A MERE TRIFLE.

Johnson. "I understand you and Baker are getting up a gold-mining company?"
Walker. "Aw—yes! Profitable bit of finance you know. You in it?"
Johnson. "No, thanks; not for me. But how are you getting on?"
Walker. "Splendidly! We've got everything but the mine!"

A "NOTE"-WORTHY TRANSACTION.

A certain jobber had a considerable number of Unified open with a well-known broker, and one contango day he asked the broker when he intended taking them up; the latter, not liking the way the question was put, said he would take them up on the account day, and if the jobber liked he would pay for them in bank notes. "Very well," said the jobber, "so you shall." On the account, the jobber delivered the stock and received 2,313 £5 notes, representing £11,565. As the notes were all nicely mixed up, it took a couple of clerks about an hour to sort them and put them in order. As every bank note is cancelled upon its return to the bank, and the cost of a note is considerable, the bankers at once traced the matter out, and altogether there was a nice little "row in the shop." The jobber prefers cheques now. It is said this joke cost the Bank about £100.

A SCARE IN THE HOUSE.

Some fine games were played upon sundry members by some very "old boys," in the old French market, who used to sit and go to sleep during the winter months, by the fire near Wetenhall's old box. A good scene of retaliation once took place, in which Harry Brown was the leading spirit. A favourite amusement used to be to fill a filbert-nut full of gunpowder, attach a tiny fuse to it, and then place it on a member's hat or on the seat close to him, when he was asleep. It used to explode, and so used he. One afternoon they played this trick on Harry Brown, who was napping after lunch. Harry Brown went out swearing they should pay for it, and, going to Isaacs (who then had a stall in Hercules Passage), returned with a large cocoa-nut, to which was attached a squib. This he laid hurriedly down in the centre of the House—in less than two minutes nearly all the members discovered that they had important engagements to keep, and bolted. The squib went on spitting and sputtering. A manager ordered "Long Annuities" (Wilkinson) to take it away, who, thinking it contained at least a pound of gunpowder, refused. So the supposed infernal machine was left to burn itself away in a nearly deserted House, which was done without any startling effects, as the nut was quite innocent of any other than its own proper contents. The members had been "done Brown."

THE
STOCK EXCHANGE ALMANACK
FOR
1856.

DEDICATED

(With or without permission)

TO

THE COMMITTEE

OF

THE STOCK EXCHANGE.

Dulce et decorum est, in causam risûs, mori.

The Authors reserve to themselves the right of Translation.

1856.

ALFRED HOBDAY, LITHOGRAPHER, ENGRAVER AND PRINTER,
56, BOW LANE, CHEAPSIDE.

STOCK EXCHANGE ALMANACK FOR 1856.

JANUARY.

1st. Bond, Idle, Backhouse drink the New Year in,
     The two in sherry, and the one in gin.
2nd. Bill Eykyn with young Rhodes begins to job,
     And no more borrows of his friends a bob.
3rd. Levien declares the Hebrew operation
     A damn'd, impertinent, mad speculation.
4th. Bummy, returning from over the seas,
     The vessel gets caught in a terrible breeze;
     The sailors, dismay'd at the boisterous gale
     (Remembering how Jonah was thrown to the whale),
     In order to rescue themselves from the squall,
     Pitch over Bummy, baggage and all.
5th. Instead of fees, for turns our Hawkins' cures;
     The profit's his—the remedy is yours!
7th. Boldly the captain addressed his papa,
     And asked his permission to go the war.
     "No, no, my beloved!" old Helbert replied,
     "Stop here and I'll find you a sweet Hebrew
      bride!"
     But Rothschild exclaimed, "Let him go if he will;
     " My son shall go with him, and I'll pay the bill!"

Remarkable Events.

General festivity. Hilar(it)y Term begins. Brandy balls invented by McGill, 1855.

Mitchell's business falls off.

Rothschild dines off Peace Pudding.

The well-known Mr. Samuels, after a prolonged sojourn in foreign parts, returns to his friends, and finds the Bottle Imp has greatly increased the business.

Consultations from 11 to 3. Bleeding practised. No advice under £3. 2s. 6d. Operations performed in the market.

The Captain wants to see Sebastopol, and objects to taking Barley. Gets a passport for Jerusalem; is afraid of being captured for a Tartar. Provides himself with a bottle of Chili vinegar.

FEBRUARY.

6th. To make things worse, it needs but A. B. Cook,
     To give the market his peculiar look;
8th. To make them better, just let Wagg walk thro',
     And better still, let Barley crawl in too.
10th. Now do the "Heavies" round the fire throng,
     And fill the air with their prophetic song.

(H)Ash Wednesday.
Too many cooks, &c.
Cope looks out for a sop in the pan. Helbert reaps a harvest. Wagg has a lunch for nothing at Mabey's. Poor clerks apply there for waiters' places.
Royal Oak 'bus refuses to take John Mocatta for a single fare.

MARCH.

1st. Spike says: "If Russia's beat, just wait a minit,
     "You call at Bedlam and you'll find me in it!"
14th. Haes says: "For Lawford I don't care a cuss,
      sir,
      "Altho' he's vigorous, the market's wusser."
23rd. The Spanish Dancers stop up extra late,
      The birthday of their Crabb to celebrate.
25th. The committee have made up their minds this
      year,
      That our friend, Louis Samson, shall fill the chair;
      For they say, whilst the business *they* carefully
         mind,
      He'll be able to jaw till he talks himself blind.

Hares let loose. Spike writes to the Czar from St. Luke's.

Windischgratz gets blown up. The jobbers raise the wind.

Lobster suppers in the Haymarket. Capture of the *Red'un*.

The Scrutineer's dinner stopped. South "declares" members in *blank* verse.

HOUSE SCRAPS.

APRIL.

1st. Auguste to many, Abraham to few,
The West-End Christian sinks the City Jew.

5th. Macbeth, when staggered by the witches hail,
Can ne'er have chanced to meet with our Dutch Mail.

22nd. Now swells return to town and throng May Fair,
And Helbert thinks his boy's the handsomest there.

28th. Now Horace, with a grave and dismal face,
Talks to you of your final resting place;
And asks his friends, who visit the Metropolis,
To spend a jolly day at the Necropolis.

30th. Worms chirps the same song thro' the livelong year—
"Vy, was ist Lyons? Vell, they are not dear!"

MAY.

2nd. Now flaunts the Aristocracy about,
Hawks his flash stones and pulls his jewels out.

21st. Symons, who water hates and never brushes,
Sees his own figure in a glass, and blushes.

JUNE.

13th. The last new member, worthiest of men,
Confides in Russell and pays two pounds ten.

24th. The managers ask all the waiters to tea,
On account of their great civility;
They present Mr. Smith with a silver hammer,
And compliment Webb on his excellent grammar.

JULY.

14th. This day the market had a rapid fall,
And—strange to say—the Lancer saw it all!

22nd. Sam Chard, entirely on his friends' behalf,
Applies to Sims to take his *autograph*.

AUGUST.

1st. Loud cries of "Greasy" do the fact proclaim,
That near this spot the "Butcher" rears his frame.

12th. The genial weather sees our Manny fly,
In summ'ry garb to taste his first eel pie!

21st. Turks fall—the old man screams; but when they rise,
Off to his easy chair our Cohen flies!

Remarkable Events.

Is discovered by his chin.
Goes to Brigh-ten to get a mut-ten shop.
War with Holland.
Gibbs' shut up.

The Chimpanzee escapes from the Zoological Gardens.

Lord Palmerston shuts up the churchyards. Horace plants flowers at Woking "in an amphitheatre surrounded by distant hills. 1,700 of the aristocracy bury themselves there." See advertisements.

Insurrection in China.
Teapot Row built, 1785.

Sweeps are lively. "Clem" goes out as Jack-in-the-Green.

Order of the Bath instituted, A.D. —

Russell, after giving his fiftieth Canada Land dinner, *slopes* to the backwoods.

Midsummer Day.
A school found for future secretaries. Chard appointed head master.

Dog Days and Dog Carts begin.
St. Swithin. *Sticky* weather.

Sims takes out a patent.

Lam(b)mas Day.
"*Meat* me by moonlight," &c.
"Buy, Buy!"

White waistcoats now begin to be looked up. Waiter struck by strange likeness between Manny and Harry Brown.
Blackcock shooting begins.

SEPTEMBER.

3rd. Now Sims, to gain the luxuries of life,
Exhibits photographs of his dear wife.

18th. Now is the dismal time of year,
And things are looking uncommonly queer;
Whilst men tell each other with mystery,
" I've had such a ripper from A. B. C.!"

22nd. Sebag vows vengeance on the vile reporter,
Who says he married the rat-catcher's daughter!
They tried to hook him, but the plot miscarried,
'Twas *Louis Cohen's* daughter that he married!

Remarkable Events.

G. Goldsmid invents a new machine for taking likenesses, and tries to photograph a joke.
Wars and rumours of wars.
The conspirators dissemble.

Fire of London, 1666.
Sebag burnt out owing to a lucifer falling on a very greasy hat of Louis Cohen's.

OCTOBER.

2nd. What soft remembrance o'er our Crooky steals,
Whene'er he hears the ditty of " Live Eels ! "

5th. Now John Mocatta finds, with great dismay,
That fat Sam Pulley's always in his way.

25th. This day we see, oh, lamentable sight !
McGill and Hawkins both uncommon tight !

Billingsgate Market opens.
What art and talent's here combined;
For Hook and Crook in one we find.

Druids driven from their woods.
*Bom*bardment of Sebastopol.

Battle of *A-gin-court*.
Chelsea Hospital Dinner.
"When doctors disagree."

NOVEMBER.

2nd. The Brighton Age to Brompton went astray,
And the near *wheeler* fell upon the way.

4th. Old Nick takes cold, resolved to keep his bed,
And sends up Uzielli here, instead.

9th. Hartridge, no chance of civic honors seeing,
Burns his blue gown and terminates his being.

11th. Sir Charles' servants all resign their place,
Because the Cook declines to say Your Grace!

13th. Now nasty men awaken all our ire,
By drying handkerchiefs before the fire.

15th. Jack Raphael gives a supper and rout,
Salt Dutch Herrings and sour-kraut;
Gingerbread, schnapps, and passover cake,
Lots of *Gals* and no mistake.

30th. Robert Johnston illuminates his nose,
And treats the market to Athol brose;
Whilst Ross, so drunk he cannot sing,
Attempts to reel a Highland fling.

Always thought to be a steady old coach.
Old and young stagers.
Emancipation of the slaves.

Carden elected Lord Mayor.
The Toastmaster takes the pledge.

Sir C. D. Crosley builds a second pagoda in his back garden, and has his carriage door widened considerably to admit his frill.

A wiper discovered.

Jewish Feast.
Helps Seymour with his articles on Exchanges in the *Daily Nuisance.*

St. Andrew's Day.
Ross a good fellow at a pinch.

DECEMBER.	Remarkable Events.
2nd. Fresh noble Lords such honor rains upon, They make our Waley, Baron Waley-gnton.	A fresh brew for the peerage.
11th. Let Waddy's victims Love's delusions shun, Things done *by Love, for love,* are seldom done.	Love takes the chair and finds he is not "among the roses."
13th. Our Thomas determined to marry, Says the Nobbler, quite sick of that life, "I'll lay you a tenner, my pippin, "You'll repent when you've once got a wife."	St. Thomas's Day. The wretched man refuses to be advised, does the deed, and gets his hair combed without the aid of a barber.
18th. This day, the market Bostock finds a teazer, So sticks a pony slily into Keyser,	Et tu Brute? (Oh, you Brute.) *Translated by Oxley.*
23rd. When pantomimic glories fill the ear, Remember that our Bottle Imp is—here!	Look to your legs!—*Times.*
26th. About this time, increas'd by Christmas cheer, The plague of boils doth usually appear.	Boxing Day. H. Brown goes to the Pantomime, dines with Anderson, and gives a grand supper to all the clowns.
31st. At last, Charles Samson, laid upon the shelf, Concludes the play, by taking off himself.	Our readers cannot congratulate themselves on the double event.

One day a certain member rushed up to his office and found that his clerk had gone out and left about £7,000 worth of cheques in his desk, so he put them in his pocket and returned to the market. He had hardly done so before his clerk came in and told him that somebody had stolen the cheques. He enjoyed his poor clerk's misery, ordering him not to show himself until they had been found. The best part of the joke came in when our jocular member found the cheques in his own pocket on going to bed. His balance was small and he felt certain that his cheques would not be paid. He did not sleep very well that night, and was up in the city at daylight waiting for the bank to open. It turned out, however, that the bankers, knowing his stability, and thinking a mistake had been made somewhere, passed his cheques. He never attempted practical jokes with cheques after this.

Another member is said to have taken a lot of cheques home one Saturday afternoon, which, as he was changing his things for cricket, he found in his pocket. It being then about seven minutes to 3, he ran downstairs, half dressed, jumped into a cab, drove as hard as he could to his bank, which he reached a few minutes past 3; as he was well known the manager took the cheques and made all square for him. This occurred many years ago, when members thought it quite grand enough to live no farther out than the "Angel" at Islington.

Another member who banked at "Martin's" for many years opened an account at the Alliance, which was closer to his office, but from force of habit went several times to "pay in" at Martin's, even after the lapse of over a dozen years.

PROGRAMME
OF A
PROPOSED PROCESSION TO ATTEND GENERAL KOSSUTH
ON HIS ENTRY INTO THE STOCK EXCHANGE.

CAPTAIN HELBERT,
WITH A BODY OF YEOMANRY TO CLEAR THE WAY.

The MEMBERS of AUGARDE'S CLUB, headed by JOHN E. PHILLIPS, Esq.

LOUIS RAPHAEL, ESQ., IN HIS STATE WAISTCOAT.

THE AUTHOR OF THE TEMPLAR.

MR. MOSCOW BROWN, WITH A LUMP OF CALIFORNIAN GOLD.

MR. LEWIS LEVI, BEARING A BUNDLE OF CHINESE TURNPIKE BONDS.

EDWARD LEVIEN, ESQ., SUPPORTING A COUPLE OF BLOOMERS.

LOUIS COHEN, ESQ., IN A CLEAN SHIRT,
ACCOMPANIED BY MESSRS. SOLOMAN SEBAG AND MOSES LEA.

MR. BUMFORD SAMUELS.

MR. E. MOCATTA, ATTENDED BY MESSRS. OLIVER AND MENDIES.

Admiral Parker and the Reefer,
WITH MESSRS. F. LEVIEN AND BOULTON, REPRESENTING THE NAVY.

H. AUGARDE, Esq.,
WITH HIS DRAWN SWORD AND A RAW LEG OF MUTTON.

MESSRS. W. EYKYN AND H. BROWN, AS A DEPUTATION FROM THE SOCIALISTS OF PARIS.

MESSRS. UZIELLI BROTHERS, WITH BANJOS.

GENERAL KOSSUTH,
ATTENDED BY
Messrs. JOHN ROSS SODEN and STEPHEN SPURLING,
AND FOLLOWED BY
THE NOBBLER,
Offering to Lay him any Odds against his Safe Arrival in America.

Allegorical Tableaux.
DISMAL JEMMIE, IN CHAINS, REPRESENTING THE CAPTIVE SPIRIT OF HUNGARY.

MESSRS. RATTON, RUSSELL, AND W. HARTRIDGE,
AS
FAITH, HOPE, and CHARITY.
MR. CHARLES MITCHELL, AS THE MAN IN ARMOUR.

MESSRS. PEAKE AND S. PULLEY,

BEARING MR. PLIMPTON ON A HOD OF MORTAR.

THE DIET OF HUNGARY,
REPRESENTED BY
MESSRS. PECKETT, FENN, ROUGEMONT, AND C. BROWN, JUN.

MESSRS. HENDRICKS AND CHARD, AS ISAAC OF YORK AND WAMBA.

MR. SAM DE SYMONS, WITH A BODY OF POLICE TO KEEP THE BOYS OFF.

Note.—The date of the above I am unable to ascertain—about 1860.

HOUSE SCRAPS.

ANALYSIS OF THE STOCK EXCHANGE.

By JOHN ROLLS.

Sold for the Benefit of the Decayed Fund. Price 1s. June, 1874.

1 Abbot	1 Day	1 Collier	Mitcham	Shanks
2 Bishops	1 (K)night	3 Cooks	Newport	Fatt
1 Chaplin	1 Mundey.	3 Coopers	Peckham	Bones.
12 Clarkes	———	2 Dyers	Rhodes	
3 Monks	2 Coates	4 Fullers	Shadwell	8 Halls
1 Nunn	1 Stocken	4 Gardiners	Southgate	2 Lodges
1 Hood	1 Tassall	3 Masons	Sutherland	1 Hutt
3 Chappells	1 Cork	1 Merchant	Sutton	3 Kitchins.
1 Pugh	1 Horne	2 Merc(i)ers	Salisbury.	
1 Temple.	1 Key, with	3 Millers		Hopps
———	5 Wards	1 Potter	1 Berry	Malt(by)
4 Kings	1 Winch	2 Skinners	1 Cherry	Porter
1 Lord	3 Jacks	6 Taylors	Elms	Perry.
1 Chamberlain	1 Birch	3 Turners	2 Flowers	
2 Chancellors	1 Billett	1 Tyler	May	Lucy
3 Barrons	1 Pulley.	1 S(ch)later	Moss	Maude
2 Squires	———	1 Pitman.	Ferne.	May.
1 Major	1 Archer	———		
4 Marshalls	2 Baumen	2 Boullys		
2 Mayors	2 Fauleoners	Strong	2 Waggs	9 Hills
1 Constable	2 Flowers	Sturdy, and	1 Witt.	1 Dale
1 Paige.	1 Forrester	Hardy.	———	1 Field
———	1 Hunter	———	5 Carrs	8 Woods.
1 Bell(e)	1 Fisher	1 Bigg	1 Carter.	———
1 Batchelor	6 Walkers	1 Little		3 Lanes
1 Swaine	1 Trotter.	2 Shorts	3 Birds	2 Warks
1 Pett.	———	3 Shorter	Dawes	2 Fenns
———	North	1 Pater	1 Drake	2 Mills.
Love	West.	1 Child	1 Jay	———
Vertue		1 Boyman	4 Martens	2 Miles
Bliss	1 Lamb	1 Dandy	1 Partridge	1 Bower
Hope	1 Bull	1 Guy	1 Pidgeon	1 Moon, and
Grace.	2 Steers	1 Tidy.	4 Robbins	3 Rays.
———	3 Shepherds.		2 Starlings	———
2 Downers		Barnett	1 Wrenn	
1 Upward	1 Branch	Banbury	2 Worms	1 Wise
1 Low.	1 Sprigge	Clapham	1 Cobb	1 Vile
———	1 Thorne	Durham	3 Foxes	1 Sly.
12 Brownes	2 Vignes.	England	1 Lyon	———
6 Grays		Jordan	Brewin	All are able to
4 Whites	1 Atter	Kent	1 Wolff	Read or
1 Green.	6 Bakers	Kew	1 Crabb	Wright a
———	6 Barbers	Lancaster	1 Dolphin	Surman in a
Chalk	1 Butcher	Millbank	1 Whiting.	Towne.
Coles	3 Butlers			
Oates.				

VILL-AKINS AND HIS DINAH.

A New Version of an Old Love Story.

Here's a Lay, for Walentine's Day.

Cum all ye magnets of the City,
    Cum all ye gents of high estate,
Cum, listen to a umbel ditty
    Of Vill-Akin and his fare mate;
In Alsop Terris she resided,
    Along the Rode wot is the New;
On hir luv Vill hisself prided—
    (Loviers she had not a few).

And though hir 'ouse was called a bad 'un,
    Vill didn't much regard all that,
For all folks say Vill's a sad 'un
    (Frale vuns like him, 'cos he's fat).
Beside, ven e'er our Vill has tin,
    Freely for his fun he pays,
Goes and stops at this 'ere den
    Days and nites, and nites and days.

Like many another wicious "old" 'un,
    Ven he wants to fan his flame,
Ain't a wile unblushing bold 'un
    Wot'll coolly tell his name;
But, in guise of a tip-top Sawyer,
    Sojourns with the norty foke,
Takes the name of a wen'rable lawyer—
    The famous judge, Sir Ed'ard Coke.

The gal with whom he last was mated
    Was knowed as well as the City Barge
Fond of getting 'tosticated—
    Could a wolley of ooaths discharge;
But the young 'un who supplanted
    Her in lustful Vill's desires,
Was a gal who should be chaunted
    By a hundred thousand lyres.

For she was as fare as Florer,
    Eyes like sorcers, wide and clear,
Hair as golden as Aurorer,
    Teeth like Ingin pearls so dear;
Fond o' dressin' in silk and satin,
    Natty boots and silky hose,
Jewell'ry—I must put that in—
    With a colour like a rose.

Vun of this 'ere beauty's pals
  (Pals she had, a reg'lar string)
Was a nob among the gals,
  Under the name of Arthur Wing.
Deep in love these rivials got,
  With this comely nymph so fare,
But she fell to Awthur's lot;
  Vill is old and has lost his hare.

Heeps of money, many a pres'nt,
  Silks and laces, and fine clo's,
Which to wimmen is so pleasant
  From a man who's led by the nose;
Lots of hinfant baby linnen,
  Frox and sox, and sich like things,
Villiam, with 'is art so winnin',
  Thort to charm this gal o' Wing's.

For a pore unhappy baby
  She 'ad bore two year agoe,
And Villiam, like a reg'lar gaby,
  Cloth'd the boy from top to toe;
Cloth'd the boy and cloth'd his mother
  In finery out of the 'Arrow Rode;
Coax'd—unlike a younger brother—
  (If this ain't art may I be blowed).

The lady guv a jovial party,
  Invited Wing and Coke to dine,
All enjoy'd themselves most 'arty:
  Coke stood grubb and Wing stood wine.
Wing grew jealous of Coke's attention
  To his gal, as he did call hir—
Hir name I do not wish to mention,
  'Cos, perhaps, it might appawl hir.

So pres'n'ly Awthur did deside
  From this 'ouse the gal to take—
Poor old Coke most bitter cried,
  Sich a charmer to forsake.
'Twas upon the Monday mornin',
  Dreer and dark, and bitter cold,
All his tender feelin's scornin',
  Vill considered he was sold.

Awthur took away his wummin,
All to keep her to hisself.
My story to an end is cummin'—
Awthur was a cunnin elf;
And the 2 like tertil doves
    Pass their time, while pore old Coke
Quietly lays down the gloves,
    Considers it a cruel joke.

MORAL.

Listen, Villiam, ere you hook it,
    To the wards of Mrs. Glasse :
Catch your hare before you cook it !
    Mind! whatever comes to pass,
Don't be daily, shameless, wasting
    All your substance, health, and means,
To eternally be tasting
    Pleasure's draft in wice's scenes.

                    A. M. A.

IMMEDIATELY AFTER THE RACE

BETWEEN

OXFORD AND CAMBRIDGE,

The following Crews will compete.

LEAN.	FAT.
J. H. Barnes	J. Barber
A. Froom	F. Greenfield
W. N. Rudge	Puckle
J. Heseltine	G. Wedd
G. Barber, Sen.	Marzetti, Jun.
C. Lucas	Seleuchin
R. J. Chappell	Wm. Scott
J. E. Smith (Stroke)	Vivian (Stroke)
R. Case (Cox.)	G. Causton (Cox.)

1872.

    A facetious member having unwittingly offended a conceited puppy, the latter told him he was no "gentleman."
    "Are *you* a gentleman?" asked the droll one.
    "Yes, sir! I am."
    "Then I'm very glad *I am not.*"

THE ARTIST'S DREAM. 1879.

In Memoriam.

TARRAL WILKINSON.

The day seems desolate, and we
    A mournful song must sing,
For *Tarral's* left his friends of old,
    And joined the " Erie ring."

David the news will hear and grieve,
    Among the Pyrenees ;
At Hamburg *Albert Cohen* will
    Shake to the very knees.

When *Lionel Cohen* learns the truth,
    Though from this spot he's far,
He'll water with his copious tears
    The hills of Penmaen Mawr.

Natty will have no heart for work,
    He'll want to "hunt" or "row;"
And *Alfred*—well, there's just a "chance"
    That he'll survive the blow.

Hardy (not gentleman) will mourn
    The unexpected wrench—
(He's crossed the Channel, so we hear,
    To learn to bark in French).

Charlesworth will feel as if caught out
    Of stocks (the market higher);
Unmanned, he'll give the jobbing book
    To *Jessie* and *Maria*.

Spiellman will cease, to some extent,
    From his "gigantic dealings;"
Sturdy will have to go away,
    Its too much "for his feelings."

Douglas will have another friend's
    Sad absence to deplore!
Giles will at once be so subdued,
    You'll scarcely hear his "roar."

Castello, solace he will find
    With his "poor wife and child;"
While *Moens*, in a mellow voice,
    Will cease to drive us wild.

> *Leon* will seek the Cuckoo's notes,
>   To charm his grief away;
> And little *Wagg*, to drown his care,
>   Will whistle all the day.
>
> *Murray*, henceforth, with naughty words
>   Will cease to plague our lives,
> And try to change his cry of " Co-
>   Hen Turks, or Turkey fives."
>
> Thus, all heart-broken, our song
>   Must be a doleful carol,
> For we have lost a valued friend
>   In our departed *Tarral*.
>   *August 16th, 1872.*

IMPROMPTU LINES.

Written on a Member quitting the Stock Exchange under peculiar circumstances.

" *Magna est veritas, et prævalebit.*"

London, *March, 1858.*

> Contangoes, options, call-of-mores,
> And various other jobber's stores,
> Of call-backs, put-backs, and a train
> That occupied his active brain,
> Are no more—at least to him ;
> His cup he filled unto the brim
> With goodly stuff, but tasted not ;
> For others was reserved the lot.
> Since some a pois'nous drug had mixed,
> By which a multitude were fixed,
> And he escaped. But who shall tell
> What dire misfortunes then befell?
> Committees, clamours, threat'ning, lying,
> And ranc'rous dealers sense defying.
> Oh! what a herd, and what a sight,
> Where all brought fairly into light !
> Long did I see a noisy crew
> Dispute about an I or U,
> Neglect inquiries of the matter,
> And spend their time in idle chatter;
> Or try, with vain and pompous threats,
> To bring a victim to their nets.

Whilst few of them, alas! could stand
The brunt of battle, hand to hand;
He stood unmov'd—but, with his friends,
Determined to maintain his ends.
And though he lost his curious trade,
By which some money can be made,
Would not fall quite a sacrifice
To malice, jealousy, or vice,
But kept his cash; which vex'd still more,
And made more angry than before,
The Stock Exchange, who, on a Board
Fit for a noble Duke or Lord,
Libel'd his name, that all might see
A martyr, willing to be free,
Who bade defiance to their laws,
When on his means they put their paws
Without fair claim. They'd done enough
To aggravate much milder stuff
Than he was made of, and attain
Themselves a Board of blacker stain.
And then, too, see that *Daily News*,
At all times ready for such stews,
With base audacity proclaim
Its creed—endeavouring to defame.
Full many a name is bought and sold,
And made—or good, or bad—by gold!
Its action seems like so much leaven,
To raise and swell our pride to heaven;
Or should it gain ungenial sway,
Evil might go the other way.
Oh! had he but unbent his mind,
And mixed more freely with his kind,
He might have learnt, when in his need,
To adopt a far more different creed;
And take " policy " to guide
His interests right and bend his pride.
Still " honor " knew of no such call,
And character must stand or fall;
So " policy " was cast aside—
By " honor's " flag he must abide!
With " truth " and " justice," and he will
In spite of all maintain them still.
How much men judge by outward show,
How far do faction's numbers go;
While little truth and reason sway
To test the bubbles of the day.

GIRAFFE
(Gun-ní)

Alas for man, were man to be
The judges of a conscience free !
Vain-glorious man, too prone to rule
And prove thyself both knave and fool,
Divest your heart of love for gold,
Let not your mind be bought or sold,
But give it freedom, and expand
Your thoughts o'er all the sea and land ;
Thus learn more wisdom, truth, and love,
From works performed by Him above,
And then a better judge you'll be,
And from temptation's curses free.

P.S.—Postcript the first—and last—I write,
My muse, in aid, must still indite,
New falsehoods have my bosom stung,
And latent truths are from it wrung ;
But critics spare me—well I know,
And could myself the errors show
In composition, not one whit
Shall now be altered, as I've writ
For facts and candour's sake, and him
Whose cup was filled unto the brim ;
When those perfidious creatures, knaves
Whose minds are to their pockets—slaves,
Destroyed it and then tried to damn him,
To frighten, or at least unman him ;
But Daniel in the lion's den
Stood not more firm than he did then,
And showed the rascals that within,
A conscience was quite free from sin,
That thus upheld him in sore trials,
Thro' many wrongs and more denials ;
Steadfast remained he—and may they
Go, look for other, easier prey ;
In search of it hold fast together,
And strip their prize of every feather.
They'll have from me—but might have worse—
My hearty hatred and my curse !
Yet, should I say so ? May not they
Deem themselves right, in their own way?
Survey the sword-fish, see the pike,
Watch sharks of th' ocean and the like,
Behold the raven, view the hawk,
The hungry bittern and the stork,

The rav'nous wolf, the cunning fox,
As well as those who deal in stocks;
And shall not bulls and bears unite
To gain their living by the fight—
The universal fight for life—
With angry words or bitter strife?
The lot designed of things created,
That appetites must all be sated,
Lest death untimely intervene
And put an end to th' earthly scene.
Then stay just satire—mind, be still,
And bow to a Superior Will.

CARMEN.

RE-PRINTED AND RE-DEDICATED TO THE MEMBERS OF THE STOCK EXCHANGE.

Rectius vives, Licini, neque altum
Semper urgendo; neque, dum procellas
Cautus horrescis, nimium premendo
                Litus iniquum.

Auream quisquis mediocritatem
Diligit, tutus caret obsoleti
Sordibus tecti, caret invidenda
                Sobrius aula.

Sœpius ventis agitatur ingens
Pinus; et celsœ graviore casu
Decidunt turres; feriuntque summos
                Fulmina montes.

Sperat infestis, metuit secundis
Alteram sortem bene prœparatum
Pectus. Informes hiemes reducit
                Jupiter, idem

Summovet, Non, si male nunc, et olim
Sic erit: quondam cithara tacentem
Suscitat Musam, neque semper arcum
                Tendit Apollo.

Rebus angustis animosus atque
Fortis appare; sapienter idem
Contrahes vento nimium secundo
                Turgida vela.

Appended is a prose translation of the above ode:—

"He who desires, Licinius, to sail with safety the sea of life, must be careful neither to defy the dangers of mid-ocean, nor, from fear of storms, to sail timidly too near the shore, and run thereby on rocks or shoals. The lover of the happy mean (more precious far than gold) shuns alike the palace and the hovel, as in neither could he find repose. The proud oak is wholly exposed to the fury of a gale; loftiest towers tumble with the heaviest crash; the tops of the most aspiring mountains are those which the lightning scathes. Amid direst distress the well-governed mind nourishes hope, and is prepared for reverses in the height of prosperity. If Jupiter sends frosts and storms in winter, he likewise disperses them in the spring. They who are sick to-day may be well to-morrow. Apollo's bow is not always stretched: but, ever and again, he attunes his lyre to awaken one of the muses. Show misfortune a firm front, and, when favouring winds blow strongly, at once take in all needless sail."

This ode is re-printed, and now re-dedicated to the members of the Stock Exchange, as one of the best bits of advice ever given in profane writings, as they are termed:—

> Rebus angustis animosus atque
> Fortis adpare; sapienter idem
> Contrahes vento nimium secundo.
> Turgida vela.

It is always in the power of the Stock Exchange, as a body, to arrest an unreasonable panic or any very daring speculation for a *fall:* but the writer is not so expert a financier as to be able to tell how the Stock Exchange can prevent an unwarrantable rise or undue inflation of prices. It is one thing to catch a bear—with certainty of not being hurt—but quite another thing to prevent a bull from tossing you if you try to baulk him.

Take, for example, any stock: the "Caledonian" for instance, which paid 6¾ per cent. dividend for 1875, and which attained 136 *cum* dividend. Would not a further fall, say from 104, be prevented, if each of the 2,000 most wealthy members of the House were but to purchase for their own investment even but a £100 to £500 stock?

A celebrated member was continually telling his clerk to draw a cheque for £10 for "P. K." One day, somebody asked him who P. K. stood for?

"Petty cash, of course, you ass!"

I am not sure if it was the same member who used to say it was "G. O."—"jolly hot."

SCENE.—*A country lane: shivering beggar has just finished relating to a well-fed bishop a long story of his misery.*

Bishop (grandly). "No doubt, my dear friend, your's is a very hard case. But other people have also their hardships. Why! you have no idea of the difficulty one has to find a good investment to pay 4 per cent."

A NEW READING OF SHAKSPEARE.

Although Shakspeare lived three hundred years ago, his genius gave him the power of foreknowledge to such an extent that he evidently looked ahead into futurity, and saw a race of men whom his lines would fit. A careful perusal of his works will satisfy the student that this is a true assertion. But it being impossible to give the ten thousand or more instances where we find men we know described, or their peculiarities hit off, we have chosen a few well-known men, and appended to their names Shakspeare's description of them:—

LOUIS WILDY . . . . "Will play the swan and die in music."
Othello, v. 2.

W. H. VANDERBILT . . "Huge hill of flesh, away!"
1st Henry IV., IV. 1.

Sir M. DUFF GORDON . "The apparel oft proclaims the man."
Hamlet, I. 3.

JOE MALTBY . . . . . "He hath songs for man or woman."
Winter's Tale, IV. 3.

JOHNNY HAWKINS . . . "The soul of this man is his clothes."
All's Well that Ends Well, II. 5.

ROKEBY PRICE . . . . "An honest man he is and hates the slime."
Othello, v. 2.

J. B. RENTON . . . . "More hair on thy chin than Dobbin."
Merchant of Venice, II. 2.

LIONEL L. COHEN . . . "A man of most unbounded stomach."
Henry VIII., IV. 2.

ED. GODEFROI . . . . "Little wit in thy bald crown."
King Lear, I. 4.

EVAN BLAKEWAY . . . "Familiar with men's pockets."
Henry V., III. 2.

K. F. BELLAIRS . . . . "Dreams he of smelling out another suit."
Romeo and Juliet, I. 4.

H. W. RUSSELL . . . . "A lean and hungry look."
Julius Cæsar, I. 2.

ALBAN E. BELLAIRS . . "A mystery? Ay, sir, a mystery."
Measure for Measure, IV. 2.

H. K. PAXTON . . . . "In the figure of a lamb."
Much Ado about Nothing, I. 1.

Baron ALBERT GRANT . "Keep that check for it."
As You Like It, IV. 1.

Sir HENRY TYLER . . . "His verbosity finer than the staple of his argument."
Love's Labour Lost, V. 1.

Sir E. W. WATKIN . . . "A little quiver fellow."
2nd Henry IV., III. 2.

HORACE FARQUHAR . . "Practising behaviour to his own shadow."
Twelfth Night, II. 5.

ARTHUR ANDERSON . . "He was a man of good carriage."
Love's Labour Lost, II. 1.

MIHILL SLAUGHTER . . "A woman's man."
Comedy of Errors, III. 2.

J—— S—— . . . . . "Rude am I in my speech."
Othello, I. 3.

W. V. CHARRINGTON . .	"Seen him at the barbers?"
	Much Ado about Nothing, III. 2.
J. S. WALKER	"There is no man speaks better."
	1st Henry IV., III. 1.
SIR ROBERT W. CARDEN	"Doth limp so tediously away."
	Henry V., IV. 1.
PERCY RICARDO . . .	"See him dressed in all suits."
	Taming of the Shrew, II. 1.
WM. ADDISON .	"We'll dress like urchins."
	Merry Wives, IV. 2.
WILLIAM ABBOTT . . .	"More flesh than another man."
	1st Henry IV., III. 3.
S. SMALLPIECE	"More than common tall."
	As You Like It, I. 3.
BARCLAY GREENHILL . .	"A handsome fellow."
	Pericles, II. 1.
ALFRED BAKER . .	"Bitter is thy jest."
	Love's Labour Lost, IV. 3.
——————? . . .	"Though I am not naturally honest, I am so sometimes by chance."
	Winter's Tale, IV. 3.

[The above was published in the *Financial News*, June 6th, 1884.]

THE GREAT O.

A member of a firm of brokers intimated that he should retire from business at the *end of the year*, as he had inherited a very large fortune in addition to the one he had made himself. The account day fell on the 30th December, when everything for the year was settled up. He however, turned up at the office on the afternoon of the 31st, to receive his share of the profits for that day.

THE STOCK EXCHANGE (ANALYZED).

By JOHN ROLLS.

"*What's in a Name?*"

Sold for the benefit of the Decayed Fund. August, 1877. *Price* 1s.

The Stock Exchange is to many a "Terra Incognita," hidden by several large buildings. We propose to give some idea of it and its members.

Its *extent* is very considerable. It contains: **Holland** (2), **Washington**, **Sutherland**, **Kent** (2), **Lancaster**, **Durham**, **Thorpe**, **Holderness**, **Ross**, **Salisbury** (2), **Oldham**, **Newberry**, **Hastings**, **Banbury** (3), **Mitcham**, **Peckham**, **Lee** (2), **Milbank**, **Southgate**, **Barnett** (2), **Clapham** (4), **Sutton** (2), one **Towne** besides; also the **Hudson**, **Jordan**, **Lea** and **Dee**; and yet only two **Miles**.

There are fifteen **Scotts**, seven **Moores**, one **Fleming**, and one **Dain**.

The *place* has been built some years, but has only one **Angle**, while its **Walls** may be seen walking about.

The Stock Exchange has only one **Tennent**.

Sometimes there is a **Gale**, then there is a **Noyes**.

Snow is to be seen, also **Sands** (Clayton), the **Moon**, and **Daly** too, but only three **Rays** are visible.

Crews may be seen after a **Collier** or a **Schiff**.

One member **Hopps** in with one **Legg** and one **Stocken** to **De Chair**. Two **Hoblyn** with two **Helps** on **Mundey Knight**, to borrow a **Smallpiece** from **Heap**.

Byers may be seen, but no sellers.

They have **Chambres**, but only two **Holmes** for members.

There is one **Marval** connected with the Stock Exchange: though all the members are continually going in and out, there is never more than one **Cumming** in.

There is one **Temple** for four **Bishops**, one **Chaplin** for three **Chappells**, and one **Pugh**, one **Prior**, three **Monks**, one **Nunn**, and five **Palmers**.

There are three **Kings**, two **Chancellors**, four **Marshalls**, one **Chamberlain**, and two **Paiges**; three **Barrons**, one **Lord**, one **Noble** (Bennett), one **Sun**, one **Knight**, with two **Squires**, and one **Buckler**, two **Mayors**, three **Shirreffs**, one **Burgess**, one **Baillie**, and one **Constable**.

The Stock Exchange is reputed wealthy, but among them they have only one **Lack** and two **Marks**, though they have a **Ballance**.

For *dress* they have only two or three **Coates**, two **Spencers**, one **Hood**, and one **Stocken**.

For *ornaments*, a **Tassell**, a **Tagg**, a **Goldring**, one **Diamond**, and a **Seal**.

For *punishment* there is one **Birch** for **Hyde** or **Hides**, and one **Brander**.

There are six **Walkers**, and for *conveyances* they have one **Landaw** and six **Carrs**.

The Stock Exchange has only one **Bell**, one **Pulley**, **Staples**, and one **Lock** with five **Wards**.

They have only one day in the week, **Mundey**, and one **Knight**; and only two winds, **North** and **West**.

There are nine **Prices** for two **Stocks** and one **Bond**.

HOUSE SCRAPS.

There are **Moores** (7), **Meadows, Downes, Woods** (9), **Hills** (10), one **Ridge**, one **Peake**, one **Holloway**, one **Narraway, Rhodes, Lanes** (3), **Warks** (2), one **Greene**, a **Greenwood**, a **Field, Greenfields** (2), **Greenhills** (5), **Friths** (4), **Fenns** (2), **Pitts**, a **Marsh** with **Reids**, one **Bridge**, and one **Strawbridge**.

There are **Mills** (3), **Halls** (7), **Barnes** with one **Barnewall**, one **Lodge** with two **Kitchins**, one **Hutt** and one **Backhouse**.

There is one **Bower** with **Flowers** (2), **Roses** (2), **Campion, Woodroffe**, and **May** (5), a **Ferne** and **Moss** (2), **Vignes, Elms, Thorne** and **Privett**.

If you look about you may find **Sheeres**, a **Winch**, a **Bushell**, a **Pott, Webbs**, three **Willes**, a **Davenport**, one **Horne** with three **Cases**. You may also discover **Chalk, Corks** (2), **Coles** (2), a **Billet**, and **Bones** (3) (**Shanks**).

Amongst the members there are two **Swaines** and one **Batchelor**, two are **Wedd**, one **Pater** with one **Child**, and one **Suckling**.

The members are not without **Hopes** (2), **Bliss** and **Vertue**; there is one **Love**, a **Chalmer**—perhaps it is **Maude**, perhaps it is **Lucy**.

Amongst the members there is one **Bigg**, one **Little**, one **Tiddy**, one **Midlane**, one **Meane**, two **Low**, one **Bland**, two **Trew**, one **Thorogood**, two **Towgood**, but one **Sloper**, one **Lohman**, and one **Wildman**.

You may hear a **Winney** or *two*, perhaps one **Bray** occasionally. Two are **Wylie**, one **Sharp**, one **Keen**, one **Sly**; one **Tidy**, one **Smart**, one **Dandy**, one **Guy**.

There are four **Daniells** and two **Solomons**, but only two **Waggs**, one **Witt**, and one **Wise**; one **Sturdy**, three **Hardy**, one **Strong**, one **Hale**, one **Haggard**; one **Greene**, nine **Brown**, six **Gray**, five **White**, two **Woolley**, two **Char'd**. To one you may say **Goodday**, to another **Weldon**, to another **Speakman**, to another **Say**, to others "**Walker**," to another **Baumann** (2), to another **Waithman**. There is one **Breuer**, and one is always **Brewin**, one always **Nutting**, and two **Fieling**. Two **Dunns**, one always **Dunning**, two always **Owen**. One is **Sadd** at **Parting**, another one **Greaves**. Happily there are only two **Boullys**, one **Craven**, and one **Rasch**. Two **Sandemans** with two **Whiteheads**, one looking **Upward** and four **Downers**.

Sometimes they have **Gaines**; one **Bowles** while two are **Fielding**, and one is **Fagg**.

One is **Fatt**, but four are **Fuller**; one **Long**, four **Short**, but two **Shorter**; one **Langenbach**, one **Lightbody**.

For food they have two **Meates, Rolls**, one **Pye-**(Smith), **Oates, Nutts**, a **Berry**, a **Peppercorne**, a **Cherry**; and for drink, **Porter, Perry**, and **Mead**.

They do not complain much, though they are never without a great many **Paines** (7) and **Boyles** (2), and often troubled with **Worms**.

The *animals* to be seen are a **Bull**, two **Steers**, a **Cobb**, a **Galloway**, one **Wheeler**, and one **Trotter**.

The *Birds* to be seen are **Starlings** (2), **Partridges, Dawes, Robins, Martins** (3), a **Swift**, a **Finch**, a **Pidgeon**, a **Jay**, a **Wrenn**, a **Drake**, and two **Birds** besides; but only one **Branch** and one **Sprigge** for them all to roost on.

There is one **Fisher**, with **De Worms**, after a **Jack**, a **Crabb**, a **Dolphin, Whiting**, and other **Fry**.

There are **Hunts** (4), after a **Lyon**, a **Wolfe**, a **Hart**, **De Wezele**, and **Fox**(es); two **Fowlers**, two **Faulconers**, one **Forrester** (Scott), and three **Archers**.

There are several **Sons** in the Stock Exchange: **Clementson, Davidson, Johnson, Jefferson, Jackson** (3), **Jacobson** (2), **Richardson** (6), **Robertson** (4), **Robson** (2), **Tomson, Thomson** (7), **Thompson** (4), **Stephenson** (3), **Wilson** (9), **Anderson** (4), **Atkinson** (2), **Coulson, Davidson, Dadson** (2), **Dawson** (2), **Dickinson, Finlinson, Ferguson** (2), **Gibson, Grievson, Haverson, Hodson, Henderson, Hodgson** (4), **Hudson, Mason, MacPherson, Mason, Nanson, Nicholson, Pearson** (2), **Paterson, Parkinson, Robinson, Tapson, Sandison, Sanderson, Simpson** (2), **Stevenson, Wadeson, Watson** (4), **Wilkinson** (10), **Christopherson, Harrison** (4), **Tomkinson, Dodgson** (2), **Janson, Nickisson, Dennisson.**

The *Painters* are represented by **Raphael** (3), **Rubens, Reynolds** (3), **Haydon, Grant** (2), and **Frith** (4).

The *Poets* by **Scott, Campbell, Gray, Thomson, Rogers, Ramsay, Fletcher, Prior, Waller, Wyatt, Pollak, Mackay, Morris,** and **Browning.**

The *Literary Writers* by **Addison, Fielding, Richardson, Ainsworth, Butler, Radclyffe, Boyle** (2), **Godwin** (2), **Aitken, Bentham, Hervey, Jeffery, Francis, Herbert** (7), **Roscoe, Ricardo.**

There is one **Merchant** and thirteen **Clarks,** nine **Bakers,** one **Butcher,** one **Cook,** one **Cheeseman,** four **Butlers,** nine **Taylors,** six **Barbers,** two **Tylers,** one **Potter,** one **Porter,** one **Carter,** three **Masons,** three **Turners,** one **Bowyer,** one **Pitman,** one **Dyer,** four **Wrights,** three **Coopers,** two **Millers,** one **Chandler,** three **Shepherds,** three **Gardners,** and thirty-three **Smiths;** ten **Morris** dancers, but only one **Harper;** three **Skinners** after a **Slaughter;** one **Hosier** (Morgan), two **Merciers,** but only one **'Atter.**

The same graceful Gait, in quite different Gaiters. *July, 1876.*

HOUSE SCRAPS.

SCENE.—*Smoking room in country hotel.*

A gentleman has been giving the company his opinion of stock brokers and their practices, saying, "they were, without exception, a lot of swindlers and rogues."

Another gentleman says, that "some *may* be a trifle dishonest, but if you want an unmitigated liar, and a downright rogue you must go to a lawyer."

1st Gentleman. "Sir! do you know I'm a lawyer?"
2nd Gentleman. "And I'm a stock broker. Let's do a drink."

Wild Goat (Ji'-Ji')

Parrot
(Cµ Di FROY)

STOCKS AND SHARES.

The creditors of the French Electric Force and Storage Company are requested to send in the particulars of their claims to the official liquidator by the 3rd Jan. next.—*Morning Paper.*

" Where is Capital's chance of return?
    As for any Joint Stock speculation;
Here's an end to another concern
    That looked likely to pay—liquidation!
Though the fund-holder's mind it appals
    To anticipate fiscal coercion,
You had best, perhaps, purchase Consols,
    Notwithstanding the risk of conversion.

Whosoever possesses a store
    In these days, is embarrassed with riches,
If so be that his wealth is much more
    Than the total amount that his breeches
Pocket's compass will serve to contain ;
    By investment afraid to be done, he
Goes about, and you hear him complain,
    Crying, ' What shall I do with my money?'

No more prospect of dividends snug!
    By the share-list, so dreary and dark, it
Is apparent that money's a drug,
    As they say upon 'Change, in the market.
All your treasure within a strong box,
    Peradventure 'twill soon come to locking;
Whilst Dame Durden cries, ' Bother the Stocks!'
    And deposits her hoard in a stocking."—*Punch,* 20/12/'84.

THE NEW STOCK EXCHANGE.

They have pulled down all the places,
And annex'd the vacant spaces,
   'Twixt the Bank and "Austin Friars;"
And if men refute my story,
Naught care I for men or glory!
   Said the psalmist, "Men are liars!"
They have dug such deep foundations,
That all previous generations
(Who have left a trace behind them)
              Have been exposed to view.
Finding weapons of the Norsemen,
With the spurs of Norman horsemen,
And some tesselated pavement,
              With æsthetic pots in blue.
Here the bones of Anglo-Saxons,
Ancestors of Smiths and Jacksons;
While beside them, skulls deride them,
              Of the enemies they slew.
Here the mighty crane's upheaval,
Of the buried earth primeval,
              Tells a tale of history.
Proving legends and the stories
Of old England's ancient glories,
              Truth allied to mystery.
They are raising such a building,
With marble wrought and gilding,
They are raising such a building,
As was never seen of yore.
For since the days of Noah, and the pinnacles of Goa,
There never was a structure of the kind raised up before.
When the last *débris* is carted,
And the scaffolding departed,
    To its lone mysterious dwelling far away;
When the cranes have all been banished,
And the other things have vanished,
    They will organize an opening-day,
For the gallant "organ-grinder,"
And the men who lead the dance,
Or beguile the fleeting moments
    With a mystic game of chance.
Throwing up the glittering shilling,
    Betting on the side it turns,
While the gay and festive bonfire,
    'Neath the sportive tosser burns.

HOUSE SCRAPS.

A CURIOUS TABLET DISCOVERED IN THE TEMPLE OF THE BULL AND BEAR, IN THE CIT-TEE DESERT.

JACKANDGUSHAPPY

And now we shall live in those marble halls,
    Realization of fables old,
With gallant array of retainers gay,
    In red collars, and hats turned up with gold.
Here will Klarkones tune the lyre,
And warble, filled with sacred fire,
        "This is a happy land."
Here "in the trunks" at Xmastide,
The pipes and tambours will be plied
        By many a skilful hand.
Here the huntsmen and the Tritons,
Who are "bulls" or "bears" of Brightons,
Will have scope for exercising,
Of the pastime never tiring,
        Tho' they're seldom without *Paine.*
(Markets either down or rising);
Or, the Caledonians leading.
Sometimes they retire for sherry,
Then returning still more merry,
        Dance their war-dance once again.

[The above was written in 1884, just before the new House was opened. I have cut a lot of it out, as it was extremely long.]

ROUND ABOUT LONDON.

"THE STOCK EXCHANGE."

So many "Dulcigno Seventy-per-Cents." had been left me by an aged female relative, that I wanted to hear "something to their advantage." I called upon a stock-broking friend in consequence. He did not seem greatly impressed with the value of the securities. Yes, they certainly "had" paid 70 per cent., but only for three months. For many years they had yielded nothing in the shape of interest. Under these circumstances they were not "quite" so much respected as Consols. For the rest, they had been issued at 40, and were rather under 4½ now.

From this, it appeared, they had fallen rather considerably, "but," said my stock-broking friend, speaking of the bonds as if they had been a confirmed invalid in the last stage of a rapid decline: "they may be a little better this morning. At any rate, I will go over to the House and see."

He left me in a small office. There were maps on the walls of half-finished railways and projected gold mines. A blue paper, giving the latest "odds"—I should say "prices"—was hanging over the mantel-piece, above a bottle of water, flanked by a couple of tumblers. I sat down and waited. Suddenly I became conscious of a noise that sounded like the ticking of the clock in the tower of the Houses of Parliament—

HOUSE SCRAPS.

47

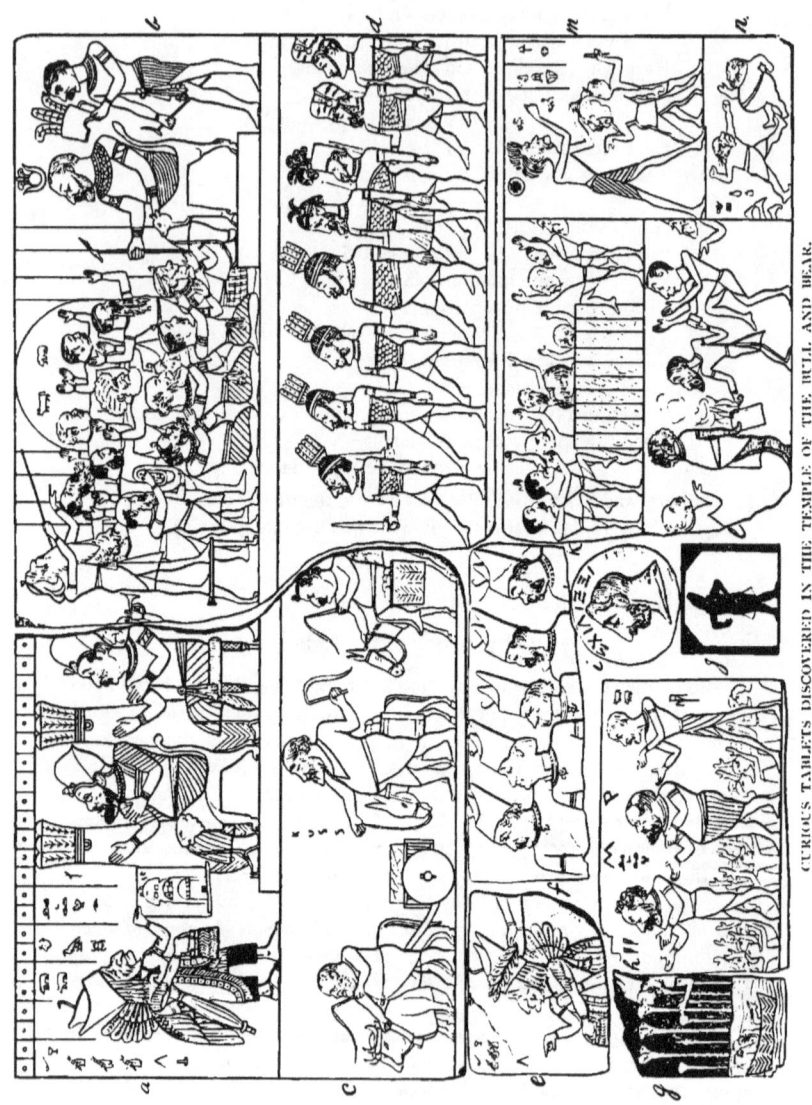

CURIOUS TABLETS DISCOVERED IN THE TEMPLE OF THE BULL AND BEAR.

exaggerated,—only it was intermittent, like the pulse of a giant suffering from indigestion. It stopped abruptly, then it began again. I traced the sounds and found that they proceeded from a little instrument, from which was issuing, by starts and jerks, a long paper tape. On the tape was printed a number of city quotations. The paper seemed to exercise a strange influence upon me. I was fascinated. It assumed all sorts of uncouth shapes. Now it rolled about like a serpent, now it enfolded me in its coils, now it fell in fanciful festoons from the ceiling. It was quite a relief to me when my stock-broking friend returned. His manner, however, was strange. He was no longer cool and collected, but very excited.

"I can see in your face," he cried, "that you want to know the mysteries of Capel Court! Well, we have been boys together, and your inmost wishes shall be gratified. I am running a dreadful risk. If I am discovered, a lingering death in the dreadful dungeons under the House will be my portion! But, no matter—come! Under my sheltering guidance you shall beard the wily stockbroker in his very den! You wear the garb of one who seems to have just quitted a band-box! In such a costume you are likely to escape observation! Once more, then—come!"

Thus earnestly addressed I could but accept his invitation. We walked down an alley, and passed through a pair of swinging doors, to meet a beadle. But the liveried guardian was no bar to our progress. We left another pair of swinging doors behind us, and were in the house itself.

It was an enormous room: white walls, bare of ornament. Here and there a desk, at which sat the dealers in Government Stock and other high-class securities; a clock, and lots of notice-boards. In the centre, a rostrum, out of which appeared and disappeared, like a figure in a Punch and Judy show, an attendant, wearing a gold-banded hat. In other parts of the building, more Punch and Judy figures of a similar character. Occasionally the puppets—I mean the officials—jumped up like jacks-in-the-box and shouted out a name. I could not help fancying that they must have taken lessons in elocution from the door-keepers of Lloyd's.

"Beadles?" I asked, in a whisper.

"No, waiters!" replied my friend, in the same tone. He took out a small book with a red binding, and hurried away. Before leaving, however, he mumbled: "no strangers admitted here, so be careful, and dissemble to the best of your ability."

I did dissemble. I placed my hands in my pockets, and, hearing that the officials were waiters, I tried to look hungry. I expected every moment to see them spring up from their recesses with plates of luscious viands, but, so far as I could see, their connection with the kitchen was as remote as possible.

Then I turned my attention to the members. I found on all sides spick and span gentlemen conversing at the top of their voices. Now and then, they adopted a lower tone: when this happened, they laughed with glee. Were these confidential utterances connected with gigantic speculations? I was full of respectful amazement. Here was I in the very centre of commercial enterprise! The spick and span gentlemen before me represented the capital of the world!

At first I was afraid to mix amongst them. But soon my curiosity conquered my timidity and I ventured to mingle with the "leviathans of commerce" while they were engaged in their gigantic operations.

Why, what was this? The leviathans—some of them Levi-Nathans—were at play. Quips, cranks, and quiddities! Business now and then in a light and airy manner, but fun first and foremost. Why, the whole place was redolent of mad ways! There was scarcely a member who was not what may be called "an amusing rattle!" Such stories! Such sparklers! Such quaint anecdotes! Who were these humorists of the east, these "*farceurs*" of the City.

A fresh surprise! Instead of stock brokers some of the members were warriors! Here was a "Captain," there a "Field Marshal," and yonder a "Count." And now I drifted into the land of riddles. What was that about "cynical C," who was "Doughy," and why such frequent, albeit complimentary, allusions to "the Ancient Lubricator?" And where was "the rat," and what was he doing? And, lastly, what could possibly be meant by "Ugly Mug" and "the Missing Link?" I was perplexed beyond measure, when suddenly there was a dead silence. Quotations and quips ceased in a moment, and the stillness was positively painful. The chief waiter (looking now like a jack-in-the-box who had taken up the profession of an auctioneer) suddenly rose from his rostrum. Heavens! had my dissembling been ineffectual, and was I now about to be publicly denounced as a traitor in the camp? In a state of suspended animation I listened for that waiter's voice. He knocked three times on a desk as if something were "Going, going, gone." The something went! It was the credit of somebody departing for ever! At all events it did not personally concern "me." A melancholy pause, and then, once more "Vive la bagatelle." "The most dramatic thing I have ever seen!" I observed to a gentleman standing near me.

The gentleman looked at me sharply, noticed that I had no red book under my arm, and shouted, "fourteen hundred." In a moment I was surrounded. The amusing rattles treated me with utmost politeness, and yet somehow I lost my hat! Profuse apologies were tendered to me, and yet I began to think it better to get towards the door! I was implored to stay, and yet I think I must have been pushed by some one from behind! But in compensation coppers were thrown at my feet, and the "fun" became fast and furious! All of a sudden it dawned upon me that I was in the centre of a ring of scoffers! the waiters rushed towards me, and—

"Hullo!" shouted my stock-broker friend, re-entering his office, "you must have been asleep! what a row you have been making!"

"Where am I?" I gasped out, "Am I safe?"

"Well, not to sell Dulcigno Seventies, they are rather flat, down to one-and-a-quarter!"

Waiving away the notion of a deal in Dulcignos, I hurriedly related my adventures.

"A dream, my good fellow," said my friend, "Not a bit like the Stock Exchange, ask any member of the House, he will tell you so!"

No doubt he was right, still the dream seemed so real that my system suffered a severe shock. I visited my doctor, and was ordered change of air. Result—a run into the country, consequently no more "rounding about town"—for the present!—*Punch*, 1st Jan., 1881.

LAYS OF MODERN LONDON.

THE BATTLE OF THE OVAL.

Calendis Novembribus Pugnatum est, MDCCCLXX.

I.

"Handsome Fred of Clapham,"*
    By his football skill he swore,
That his belov'd Stock Exchange
    Should win a game once more.
By his football skill he swore it,
    And named the playing day,
And bade his messengers ride forth,
East and west, and south and north,
    To summon his array.

II.

"Ye committee and ye members
    Of Lloyd's, the far renowned,
The Stock Exchangers challenge you,
    To meet on the Oval ground;
And if ye still be stubborn,
    And fear with us to play,
Ye shall be known as sluggards,
    For ever, from this day."

III.

Then spake gigantic Roby,
    He spake a bitter jest:
"The House has sent a message
    To Lloyd's exalted nest,
Now yield thou up thy glory
    Unto the House so brave;

---

* Fred. Soden.

HOUSE SCRAPS.

Or, come forth valiantly and strive
    Thine old renown to save.
So let us to the Oval hie,
    And meet them face to face,
Our men, I ween, will there be seen,
    Each in his proper place."

IV.

Ho! hansoms, drive your fastest,
    Ho! peelers, clear the way,
The rivals ride in all their pride
    To Kennington, to-day.
All business is neglected,
    Both houses are quite thin,
Money-grubbers are dejected,
    Who think of nought but tin.

LION (WIL·Y·UM J. L..)

V.

Each side sports its colours,
    In mauve and orange clad,
The Stock Exchangers fancy their
    Appearance not so bad.
On the other hand
A stalwart band,
In dark-blue stand,
    All men, with ne'er a lad.

VI.

Not without secret trouble
    Our captain saw his foes,
For backed by fourteen stalwart men,
    The mighty Harper rose.
The game commenced at three o'clock,
    At half-past four 'twas ended,
And our side say, the others' play,
    Was much to be commended.

VII.

Now on each side the captains
    Give the signal for the fray,
And Lloyd's "kick off" the oval ball,
    The object of the day.
The Stock Exchange elected,
    Scarce knowing what to do,
Remembering Nelson's maxim,
    "Scrag every man in blue."

CAMEL (Rumdifilius Militaris)

VIII.

The fun grows fast and furious;
    I see a moving mass
Of arms and legs, and heads and feet
    (A varied "mixture," very neat,
Very "hot," but not so "sweet")
    Standing, or "gone to grass."
Luscombe gave "Bunny" Chinnery
    A very vicious hack,
And Smith gave "handsome Fred" a trip
    Which laid him on his back.

IX.

And now the game begins to spread,
    And, running in his pride,
Big Luscombe comes towards us
    With Chinnery by his side.
Chinnery running jauntily,
    Chinnery, our little "pug,"
Chinnery dash'd at Luscombe,
    And put on him "the hug."
He whirled the giant through the air,
    Full paces five or more;
I heard the crash,
I saw the smash,
    I trow, his bones are sore.

X.

But hark! the cry is "Soden!"
    And, lo! the ranks divide,
And "handsome Fred" of Clapham,
    Comes with his stately stride.
In beauty clad, a comelier lad,
    I wis was never seen,
Than "handsome Fred," the "go-a-head,"
    The pride of Clapham Green.

XI.

He smiled upon the Lloydites,
    A smile serene and high;
He looked down on his own side,
    And scorn was in his eye.
Quoth he, "our stout opponents
    Stand savagely at bay,
But will ye dare to follow,
    If Soden clears the way?"

XII.

He rush'd into the struggle;
    He strove with might and main;
Thrice thought he was victorious,
    Was thrice repulsed again.
We did not flinch,
But inch by inch
    The Lloyd's men made their way.
How well, men said,
Great Roby play'd,
When then he made
    The first "touch-down" that day.

SECRETARY BIRD (er- liveen)

XIII.

Now Smith advances to the front,
    The man who kicks so straight;
The Stock Exchangers hold their breath,
    And dread th' impending fate.
The ball, well-kick'd, comes—oh! too nigh
And, speeding onwards, seems to fly.
The Lloydites raise a joyful cry,
    Their triumph now is great.

XIV.

We then began another game—
Alas! our fate seemed just the same—
    Our gallant captain* fought
With all the will,
With all the skill,
    That could to it be brought.
Two glorious "runs" for us he made,
With science, power, and pluck he played;
And all our men then present said,
        "Our hopes begin to rise."
When Mackinlay, by a splendid "run,"
    Has passed our players one by one,
Lloyd's second goal that day has won,
        And is lauded to the skies.

XV.

And now the game is over,
    Lloyd's men have fairly won
Two goals unto our nothing,
    In truth, it was well done!

    * George Strachan.

Wild Bull Dog (fac)

And so they've hied them back to town,
With victory's immortal crown;
And by their play,
Throughout the day,
Have kept their old renown.

XVI.

Poor Chinnery, our favourite "pug,"
    I fear came off but ill;
He has a blister on his foot,
    'Twould take a pint to fill.
His "dexter ogle" has a "mouse,"
    His "conk's devoid of bark,"
The "off-side" of his "kissing-trap"
    Displays an ugly mark!

XVII.

" Here's honour and prosperity
    To Lloyd's exalted nest;
With honour and prosperity
    May our Stock Exchange be blest;
May many another game be played,
    More even may they be;
May Heaven grant us the victory,
    And send me there to see!

FINIS.

THE NEW STOCK EXCHANGE.

The members pouring inwards,
    A concourse bright and gay;
Our Capitol was crowded—
    It was Contango day.
But the pushing and the crowding
    Made it fearful work to see,
While the rushing and the crushing
    Raised the question, Shall this be?
So the fathers met in council,
    And they tightly closed the door;
While they swore that ancient Romans
    Should be vandalized no more.

    *   *   *   *

Great *Laurentius* and *Rentonius*,
    With *Cohenus*, all were there;
Yea, they swore, like ancient Romans,
    They would hear the Romans' prayer.

HOUSE SCRAPS.

Cohenus first outspeaking:
"Oh! my comrades, list to me,
Now who will stand old Rome in stead,
And build a house with me?"
Then outspake brave *Laurentius*,
An honest man was he,

THE STOCK EXCHANGE
MAY 1887

"Lo! I will stand at thy right hand,
And run the bills with thee."
And up arose *Scruttonius*,
A vet'ran tried and free,
"E'en I will 'bide close by thy side,
And lay the plans with thee."
"Oh! Captains," quoth our Consul,
"As thou say'st, so let it be;

And we'll build as old *Cohenus*
   Shall order it to be."
Scruttonius, in the struggle,
   Spared neither lands nor gold;
He feared no might, but fought for right,
   Like Horatius did of old.
They raised a mighty structure
   Of marble, near the site
Where the fathers met together
   In the Capitol at night.
And now, with shouts and clapping,
   And cheering, long and loud,
They enter, with *Cohenus*
   Borne by the joyous crowd.
Raise high a Trojan column,
   Go, sculpture round its shaft,
In one long, grand procession,
   The masters of our craft—
Laurentius and *Cohenus*,
   Scruttonius in their rear,
Clarkensis and *Cardensis*,
   With the men who knew no fear!
Place it in the Comitium,
   Plain for all folks to see,
Cohenus, in his harness,
   Halting upon one knee;
While underneath is written,
   In letters all of gold,
How well *Colenus* built the House
   In the brave days of old!

[The above was written by an old member when the new building was opened, in January, 1885.]

HAD HIM THERE!

Late one night a certain jobber was waiting at the station to go home, but when the train came up it was crammed so full that he could not find a seat anywhere. At last a brilliant idea struck him. Going up to a first-class compartment, he looked in and then called the inspector, and said, "I say, guard, there is a man in here with a second-class ticket." The inspector examined the tickets, and actually did find a mild-looking youth with a second-class ticket; so he made him get out, and our jobber at once took his place. Just as the train was moving out of the station, and he saw the unfortunate youth left on the platform, he whispered, "I guess I had him there, I've got a *third*.'"

THE STOCK
From "The Illu...

;HANGE, 1844.
d London News.

A STRANGER'S VISIT TO THE HOUSE.

Some people imagine that it is impossible for an "outsider" to get into the House without being noticed, whereas nothing is easier. It is true that the waiters are always on the alert to prevent anybody not connected with the House from getting through the doors, but, with upwards of four thousand members and clerks, it is impossible for them to know everybody in the House—being stationed at separate doors all the year round, there must be a fair proportion of members whom some never see. A jobber in the Unified market is a comparative stranger to even many of the members in the Consol or American markets. If a man, with nothing peculiar about his appearance, and with a few papers in his hand, walked up to one of the busy doors, he could easily pass through without fear of being stopped. When an

FOURTEEN HUNDRED! WHERE IS HE?

"outsider" *is* noticed, the waiters remove him before the members have time to play any pranks upon him. In the good old days (when brokers gave turns), if a stranger did manage to effect an entrance, he was nearly always roughly handled, and was glad to escape from the clutches of the members. The following account, written by a gentleman who paid a visit to the House many years ago, has appeared in several magazines. The writer appears to have lost his way, and, observing some people congregated round one of the entrances to the House, to have walked through the door to see what was going on. He says:—" I turned to the right and found myself in a spacious apartment, which was nearly filled with persons more respectable in appearance than the crew I had left at the door. Curious to see all that was to be seen, I began to scrutinise the place and the society into which I had intruded. But I was prevented from indulging in the reflections which began to suggest themselves by the conduct of those about me. A curly-haired Jew, with a face as yellow as a guinea, stopped plump before me, fixed his black, leering eyes full on me, and exclaimed, without the slightest anxiety about my hearing him.

"'So help me Got, Mo, who is he?'

"Instead of replying in a straightforward way, Mo raised his voice as loud as he could, and shouted with might and main:

"'Fourteen hundred new fives!'

"A hundred voices repeated the mysterious exclamation.

"'Fourteen hundred new fives! Where? where? Fourteen hundred new fives! Now for a look! Where is he? Go it, go it!' were the cries raised on all sides by the crowd, which rallied about my person like a swarm of bees. And then Mo, by way of proceeding to business, repeating the war-cry, staggered sideways against me so as to almost knock me down. My fall, however, was happily prevented by the kindness of a brawny Scotchman, who, humanely calling out 'Let the man be,' was so good as to stay me in my course with his shoulder, and even to send me back towards Mo with such violence that, had he not been supported by a string of his friends, he must infallibly have fallen. Being thus backed, however, he was able to withstand the shock and to give me a new impulse in the direction of the Scotchman, who, awaiting my return, treated me to another hoist as before, and I found these two worthies were likely to amuse themselves with me as a shuttlecock for the next quarter-of-an-hour. I struggled violently to extricate myself from this unpleasant situation, and, by aiming a blow at the Jew, induced Moses to stay his next hit and to allow me for a moment to regain my feet.  The rash step which I had taken was likely to produce very serious consequences. All around me grew exasperated. The attack was resumed with greater fury than ever. Each person about me seemed desirous to contribute to my destruction, and some of their number feelingly shouted, 'Spare his life, but break his limbs!'

"My alarm was extreme, and I looked about anxiously for a means of escape. 'You ought to be ashamed of yourselves to ill-use the gentleman in that fashion,' squeaked a small, imp-like person, affecting sympathy, and then trying to renew the sport. 'How would you like it yourself if you were a stranger?' remarked another, shaking his sandy locks, with a knowing look, and knocking off my hat as he spoke. I made a desperate blow at the villain. It missed its aim, owing to the expeditious retreat he effected, and I had prudence enough to reflect that it would be more advisable to recover my hat than to pursue the enemy. Turning round, I saw my unfortunate beaver, or 'canister' as it was called by the gentry who had it in their keeping, bounding backwards and forwards between the Caledonian and his clan and the Jew and his tribe. Covered with perspiration, foaming with rage, and almost fainting from heat and exhaustion, I at last succeeded in regaining possession of my unfortunate head-piece. I did not dare to reinstate it, but was forced to grasp it firmly with both hands to secure it from further rough usage. I baffled several desperate snatches, one of which carried away the lining, and was now trying to keep the enemy at bay; afraid to again attack the host arrayed against me, but not knowing how to beat a graceful and orderly retreat, when a person, who had not made himself conspicuous, approached and interfered : ' Really, you had better go out!' pointing, as he spoke, to a door I had not seen before."

Lord Chatham was once kind enough to speak of stock jobbers as the "cannibals of Change Alley." "To me, my Lords," he once said, "whether they be miserable jobbers of Change Alley or the lofty Asiatic plunderers of Leadenhall Street, they are equally detestable."

A prominent member, who thought he would like to take a seat in the House of Commons, therefore did his utmost to secure the goodwill and votes of a constituency. In speaking, he generally got a little mixed in his literary references. On one occasion he said: "Could the liberal party ever be destroyed, depend upon it, like the *sphinx*, *it would rise at once into life again from its own ashes.*" Another time, he grew so eloquent upon the firmness of his party as to inform his audience that "the roots of liberalism are firmly planted in *terra cotta.*" And once again, he wound up the proceedings by proposing "that the meeting be adjourned *sine qua non.*"

A prominent member, whilst being shown over a picture gallery, thought it the proper thing to talk about paintings and painters. He met a friend, who asked him what he was doing in a picture gallery, as he did not know a good picture when he saw one. Our prominent member got very cross, and begged to inform his friend that he was "a conooser."

A young jobber had been spending the evening with a friend who lived in good style, and had a beautiful house in a northern suburb. As he was leaving to catch his last train a tremendous storm broke out, and, naturally enough, his host pitied him for having to turn out in such a wretched night. The jobber said, he did not need to be pitied. "Why, my dear fellow ! I am really better off than you are, *I've* got a home *to go to*, and *you* haven't."

Two members were discussing the relative merits of their pointers. One said *his* dog was so clever that it would not go out with him unless his cartridges fit his gun, &c. "Well, old man, I must admit that your dog is above the average, but I'll back mine against him for a fiver. I was in our lane the other evening, when my dog pointed a man I had never seen before, and as nothing would make him move, I went up to the man and said, 'Sir, would you oblige me with your name?' 'Yes, sir, my name is Partridge.'"

HOUSE SCRAPS.

Old B. B. W—— was very rich, and was also a bit of a screw. One day he told a friend that he was "poor, but honest." His friend replied, "Bravo, sir! two lies in three words isn't bad for you."

"THE GREAT TUM."

BULL OR BEAR.

A man was complaining that he had lost all his money through gambling on the Stock Exchange. A friend ventured to ask him if he had been a "Bull" or a "Bear?" and was told, "Neither; I was an ass."

A jobber of Semitic origin, who had only recently entered the House, accosted a fellow member who had suffered reverses. "Mishter Bobbs," he said with an insinuating smile, "I understand you don't lock up sho much shtock as you ushed to, have you got any old security boxes to disposh of? I'll make you a firsh rate bid for 'em, s'elp me never." He was offered one box, but managed to duck, and got away as fast as possible.

TALENT.

It was the time of the Turkish panic. A wealthy jobber, in whose veins flowed a mingled stream of European and Asiatic blood, offered "Twenty Turks at 19½!" A youthful broker (with more energy than capital) eagerly said, "Yes!" The jobber looked mournfully at him, and then mysteriously beckoned him into a corner.

"Loog 'ere, ole shap!" he whispered, in an agitated voice, "you are a young man, and I do not like that you should lose your money, zo I dink it is right for me to tell you (in de sdrictest confidence of corse, ole shap!) dat I am not all right. I vill sgratch de bargain if you wish, for I do not vant to damage you."

The youthful broker gratefully pressed the hand of that mournful jobber, and scratched the bargain. As he turned away he heard the market frantically bidding 20 for Turks. "Confound it!" he said to the jobber, "I've lost my market." But the jobber only wrung his hands in grief, and hastily wiping a tear from the nearest eye with the cuff of his coat, disappeared into the crowd. When the morning of the account day arrived that youthful broker was hammered, amongst many others. When the jobber heard the name announced he "vinked" to his clerk and proudly said, "Dat is vat I call talent; I have saved a thousand quids." Turks made up at 14½ that account.

WHO "VINKED."

The same jobber on another occasion offered a large amount of stock in the market, but as he was banging, another dealer snapped him immediately. "You are too late, my vrend," coolly replied the jobber, pretending to book a bargain. "But I took your stock," protested the other, "no one else opened his mouth."

"Ah! but somebody vinked."

"Who was it?" was asked on all sides.

"I cannot expose my client's business," the astute one responded.

The man who "*vinked*" has been advertised for, but he has not yet turned up.

It is reported that a prominent member—who, by-the-bye, has made a "big pile"—went to school but three times in his life, and then it was only to a night school. Two nights the teacher didn't come, and the third night he forgot to take a candle and couldn't see.

A SHOOTING PARTY.

Three members, who looked upon themselves as the three best shots in the House, were talking about some of their wonderful performances with guns at different times. As it seemed rather doubtful which could be the best shot of the three, they arranged a match for twenty birds each, at 40 yards. One other member was also allowed to enter, but as he was not reckoned much of a marksman he was allowed two birds. The important day arrived; all the arrangements were carried out to perfection; each

The Rajah amongst the Longtails.

man asked numerous friends to come to see him win. The birds were let loose. The noble sportsmen fired away with vigour, but, strange to say, not any of the competitors managed to even wing one, so when all the birds had settled on the neighbouring trees, the rivals, with a quaint expression in their eyes, of laughter and sorrow mixed, declared the outsider winner by the *two birds* that had been *given* him.

It is said that a well-known speculator down Wall Street is sometimes so absorbed in mentally working out his gigantic schemes, that on one occasion he began sharpening one of his fingers in mistake for a pencil, and only found out his mistake when he was finishing off the bone.

Two members were racing down the Ripley Road one Saturday afternoon on a "Humber" tandem, and, when going about sixteen miles an hour, something broke. The machine stopped dead, but the riders continued their mad career, one getting an opportunity of closely inspecting the ditch, and the other, after turning a graceful somersault, landing on his feet—much to the astonishment of an old lady who happened to be passing, and who solemnly said, "Don't you think it's rather dangerous getting off that way?"

Mr. Pyemont takes his fish, which he sends to Her Majesty.
1876.

An unconscious authority upon trade depression as the result rather than the cause of financial depression appears in the person of a waiter at Delmonico's Hotel, New York. He is said to have replied to the following question : "Joseph, everything seems unusually quiet here to-day; what's the matter with business?" "Oh! that's always the way in a bear market. The bears don't spend no money. But the bulls, they're livers. When the market goes their way they buy big dinners. Why, one of them came in last winter when the market was going up and spent thirteen or fourteen dollars for his lunch! I guess the bears have got the dyspepsia, for they can't eat nothing even when stocks are going down."—*Pall Mall Gazette*, January 28th, 1885.

THE SPECULATOR.

The night was stormy and dark, The town was shut up in sleep; Only those were abroad who were out for a lark, Or those who'd no beds to keep.

I passed through the lonely street, The wind did sing and blow, I could hear the policeman's feet, Clamping to and fro.

There stood a potato man, In the midst of all the wet; He stood with his 'tater can, In the lonely Haymarket.

Two gents of dismal mien, And dank and greasy rags, Came out of a shop of gin, Swaggering over the flags.

Swaggering over the stones, These shabby bucks did walk, And I went and followed those seedy ones, And listened to their talk.

Was I sober or awake? Could I believe my ears? Those dismal beggars talked, Of nothing but railroad shares.

I wondered more and more. Says one, "Good friend of mine, How many shares have you wrote for, In the Diddlesex Junction line?"

"I wrote for 20," says Jim, "But they wouldn't give me one." His comrade straight rebuked him, For the folly he had done.

"Oh, Jim, you are unawares Of the ways of this bad town; I always write for 500 shares, And then they put me down."

"And yet you got no shares," Says Jim, "for all your boast." "I would have wrote," says Jack, "but where's The penny to pay the post?

"I lost, for I couldn't pay, That first instalment up. But here's 'taters, —smoking hot—I say, Let's stop, my boy, and sup."

And at this simple feast, The while they did regale, I drew each ragged capitalist, Down on my left thumbnail.

Their talk did me perplex; All night I tumbled and tost, And thought of railroad specs, And how money was won and lost.

"Bless railroads everywhere," I said, "and the world's advance; Bless every railroad share In Italy, Ireland, France; For never a beggar need now despair, And every rogue has a chance."—*Thackeray.*

There was a shooting party in Surrey a few days ago. The party, six in number, were all "gentlemen from the City." They used enough E. C. powder to generally raise the trade depression: but at lunch time they had only killed *one* bird, which a retriever dog which accompanied one of them ate upon the spot. About three o'clock the keeper's face became very solemn, and at four, unable to stand it any longer, he exclaimed, in a growling voice, "May be, if I brawt a few o' my tame rabbits up from the hutch, you gents *'ud have some sport.*"—*Vanity Fair.*

WINE IS A MOCKER.

The career of Sir Benjamin Bobber,
    A man of financial repute,
Better known as the demon stock jobber,
    And eke, as Sir Ben the astute.

I'm one of those singular creatures
    The world doesn't every day see;
Men say they detect in my features,
    A clearly-defined £ s. d.

While yet in my cradle I rested,
    They say I with stocks was bewitch'd;
As a child in New Threes had invested,
    Bought Consols before I was breech'd.

As with gathering years I grew older,
    My soul took a loftier range,
Pari passu, I yearly grew bolder,
    Became a great man upon 'Change.

Now, in Preference, Share and Debenture,
    There's no such investor as I;
There's no spec in which I wouldn't venture,
    No shares that Sir Ben wouldn't buy.

In Oregon, Wabash, Brazilian,
    Argentine, Hard Dollar, Grand Trunk,
From twenty to thirty-odd million
    Sir Benjamin Bobber has sunk.

Of bonds I've a neat cornucopia,
    I've shares in a flying balloon,
Hold all kinds of stocks in Utopia,
    Have paying concerns in the moon.

    *   *   *   *   *

I was in for some grand speculation,
    To the tune of a million or more,
And was lost in abstruse calculation,
    When a voice scream'd out "Ben, how you snore!"

The candle burns low in the socket,
    Poor Ben's from his pinnacle hurl'd;
For I havn't a cent. in my pocket,
    Nor the price of a dram in the world.—*Scraps*, 1885.

A public or a private robber,
A statesman, or a South-Sea jobber.
Swift on Poetry.

In the ivory gate of dreams
Project Excise and South-Sea schemes.
Swift on Poetry.

Mean sons of earth, who on a South-Sea tide
Of full success, swam into wealth and pride.
Young's Love of Fame.

What made directors cheat in South-Sea year?
To live on venison when it sold so dear.*
Pope's Moral Essays.

A PROMOTER'S LAMENT.

Oh! the public's grown too wary,
   'Tis in vain I now promote;
Even clergymen are chary,
   And won't help my projects float.
Widows, likewise, are too clever
   To invest their little all;
Vain, oh, vain is my endeavour,
   None will answer to my "call."
      Just my luck!
      Just my luck!

I begin to promote,
   And I end with a sigh:
I begin then to gloat
   And I finish with a cry;
I try to be gay—
   A Stock Exchange buck,
But I'm done every way;
   Oh, it's just my luck!
Truth, Christmas Number, 1883.

CHEAP RAILWAY TRAVELLING.

At a meeting of shareholders of the Grand Trunk Railway of Canada, held at Cannon Street Hotel, October 25th, 1885, the president, Sir Henry Tyler, stated that the "emigrant traffic, which was formerly an important part of our business, has been nearly destroyed in consequence of the Pennsylvania Co. carrying emigrants from New York to Chicago—a distance of 963 miles—for 4s. (1 dollar).

* In the extravagance and luxury of the South-Sea year, the price of a haunch of venison was from £3 to £5.

Mr. FRANCIS BAILY, F.R.S., the astronomer, retired from the Stock Exchange in 1825. In 1838, in the garden of his house, Tavistock Place, Russell Square, was constructed a small observatory, wherein Mr. Baily repeated the "Cavendish experiments," the Government having granted £500 towards the expense of the apparatus, &c. This was the building in which the earth was weighed, and its bulk and figure calculated; the standard measure of the British nation perpetuated; and the pendulum experiments rescued from their chief source of inaccuracy. Mr. Baily died, president of the Astronomical Society, in 1844.—*Timb's Curiosities of London.*

When we were Boys together.—*January, 1877.*

HORACE SMITH, the novelist, in conjunction with his brother, James Smith, an attorney, wrote the celebrated series of burlesques of the styles of poets, famous and popular, in 1812, well known as "Rejected Addresses." The book went through 24 editions. James wrote no more, but Horace to the last amused himself with literature.

"Is it not odd," Leigh Hunt wrote of him to Shelley, "that the only truly generous person I ever knew, who had money to be generous with, is a stock broker! And he writes poetry too—he writes poetry and pastoral dramas, and yet knows how to make money, and does it, and is still generous."

List of stock brokers who were tenants of the Royal Exchange at the time of the fire, 10th January, 1838.

Cornhill, South Gate—No. 93, J. R. Durrant,
94, Capel Curel & Cundy.
Threadneedle Street, north side—Broughton & Grinstead.
Palmer & Hope.
Threadneedle Street, North Gate—James Watson.
West Gate—Sutton, Son & Grible,
John Foster & Son,
Joseph Davis,
De Bague & Holmes,
Robert Peake.
Description of the New Royal Exchange, &c.
EFFINGHAM WILSON, 1844.

THE GOVERNMENT BROKER.

What would the Government do without its broker? There never is a difficulty in the money market but he generously comes forward, and spends his £15,000 or £20,000 with no more concern than a school-boy would drop his half-penny at the nearest apple-stall. This he does, not merely one day, or a couple of days, but he will go on buying for weeks and weeks together. He is the financial physician to the State, and no sooner does the Government feel a little tightness in its chest, than the Government broker is ready to relieve it by immediately applying for an investment, the happy application of which to the part affected enables the patient to exclaim, with as much saltatory glee as the dressing-gowned invalid in George Cruikshank's pictorial advertisement, "Ha! Ha! Cured in an instant!" He is the best friend the old lady in Threadneedle Street ever had, and, supposing that elderly female ever took it into her head to marry, we should not at all wonder at the Government broker being the object of her affections. His wealth must be something enormous, considering the amount he spends in the course of the twelvemonth; and his frugality must be almost as great as his wealth, for we notice that he never buys for any other purpose than that of paying into the savings banks. He must make money very fast, or else has an enormous "ready cash" business, that brings him in thousands every week throughout the whole year, inasmuch as it is a stereotyped fact that the Government broker limits his operations generally to buying, for you rarely catch him selling. This is a proof of the sure principal upon which he always conducts his business, and the consequence is, that the interest which accrues is invariably not less sure than the principal.

The wonder that takes our breath is, how a man who commands so much wealth, and scatters so much good wherever he scatters his gold, should have remained so long unknown? Is it not curious that the British Association, which amuses itself in solving some of the most abstruse

HOUSE SCRAPS.

mysteries of science, as connected especially with commerce, should not have raised some inquiry as to the name of this large public benefactor? A little investigation into his character would have well repaid philosophic curiosity. Seemingly, he is one of those pure-minded philanthropists, who do good by stealth, and would blush to find it fame. He must be a large-hearted, open-handed individual, whom we confess we should like extremely to know. It is not often you meet with a man who is so rich, and, at the same time, so liberal. But a few capitalists in the City are so colossal in their dealings, and yet so modest; we cannot recall to mind another millionaire, who does so much good in his golden way, and nevertheless does it so quietly, as our friend (if he will only allow us to call him) the Government broker. May he always be buying another £15,000.—*Punch*, October 8th, 1859.

JOINT-STOCK RIVER BANKS.

The banks of the Thames are rich in deposits, forming wealth of which the quantity is immense. In the event of a panic being created by typhus or cholera, it may be well to bear in mind that these banks are constituted on the principal of unlimited liability.

Punch, July 3rd, 1858.

THE SICK MAN IN THE MONEY MARKET.

Call the Turk, if you like it, the sickest of men,
    And boast Frank than Mussulman wiser;
But I'd give *him* more rope than I would to the Pope
    To the Czar, or his neighbour, the Kaiser.
Any one of the three I should just like to see,
    On our Stock Exchange coolly descending—
Soldier, priest or civilian—to ask for four million,
    And find thirty ready for lending!

Punch, April 12th, 1863.

MONEY MARKET AND CITY IDYL.

The January dividends
    Will now be shortly paid.
His money to the State who lends
    To lose is nought afraid.
But O! how very small the rent,
    Though certain it may be,
Whereof the fundholder, per cent.
    Receives no more than three.

So little were enough to make
    That man, Bank Stock who owns,
Go sell it out, and, wide-awake,
    Invest in Turkish loans
Of six per cent., because thereby
    May dividends be had,
But oh! where interest is high,
    Security is bad!

Suppose that into joint-stock shares
    My capital I cast,
How stand the company's affairs?
    How long will sunshine last?
Concerns of highest name oft fall,
    Then cash is worse than fled,
Each being liable for all,
    Unless they're limited.

At present gas is paying well,
    But there's an awful doubt,
How soon may be, ah! who can tell,
    New source of light found out?
When I should bray an' 'twere an ass
    Demented by the moon,
Beholding all my worth in gas
    Collapse like burst balloon.

Ye banks, ye railways, and ye mines
    Ye speculations all,
I watch your fluctuating signs,
    Your prices rise and fall,
O! would that I had clairvoyance
    To penetrate the veil,
See which of you defies mischance
    And which of you will fail.

HOUSE SCRAPS.

Some are, among e'en men on 'Change,
Who credit spirits' knocks,
Lie out of their familiars' range
The secrets of the stocks?
Alas! no medium can be found
'Mongst all of the possessed,
To say what are and are not sound
And guide me to invest!

Punch, January 11th, 1873.

HOUSE COLDS AND DRAUGHTS.*

Oh! most grave and revd. seniors,
In these days of rails and wires,
Cease your engineering scheming;
Give us back our sea-coal fires.
Draughts and currents now surround us,
Coughs and asthma kill our braves,
So your knavish tricks confound us,
Carry us to early graves.
Oh! just won't the noble savage
Of Macaulay shake his head,
Won't he smile at this invention,
In the city of the dead;
Then he'll mourn departed members
In their fam'ly vaults confined,
Immolated on the altar
Of our building marble-lined.

BEARS ALL.

"Great war-panic on the Stock Exchange. . . . . All Russian securities had a heavy fall."—*Evening Paper*, Wednesday, October 18th.

Brokers and jobbers ought to thank
Their friends, Lord Beaconsfield and Derby,
For last week's treat—so near the Bank—
Unusual treat, of " rus(s) in urbe."

Punch, October 28th, 1876.

---

* In the New Building open fires were done away with, and a system of heating by pumping warm air into the House was tried; and during the latter months of the winter 1884-5, and also during the whole of the winter 1885-6, the system was not successful. The draughts were very bad, and many members were laid up in consequence. Many men wore thick overcoats all day, and even then were compelled to jump about to warm themselves—others used to run round the building and try various tricks to warm their half-frozen joints. Great improvements were afterwards made.

HOUSE SLANG.

Oh! in the days of old,
At least, so I've been told,
We only heard of "*puff*," and "*rig*," and "*bang*,"
But now better things exist,
For we daily swell the list,
And have really quite a choice of market slang.
We'd a "*fiddle*" then, it's true,
But our "*puts*" and "*calls*" were few,
Of words that appertain to "*Bull*" or "*Bear:*"
Now we've daily something new,
And we've really quite a crew
Of fancy names to represent a share.
I hope I shall not stray
From virtue's narrow way,
Or find myself " at sea " in wild verbosity;
But fancy, by-the-way,
Now, in the present day,
A Varna's a "*Bulgarian atrocity.*"
So now we shall soon have our "*Crackers*,"
And likely enough our "*Cheroots*,"
While our "*Bones*" can be sent to the "*Knacker's*,"
And then we have sweet "*Sarah's Boots.*"
We beat Charlie D—— and Lord Byron
In their nice, gay Lotharian ways,
For we have our "*Sarahs* ' and "*Claras*,"
Our "*Noras*" and "*Doras*" for fays.
We kneel at the feet of our "*Nancy's*,"
We load them with "*Cottons*" and "*Tapes;*"
If anything tickles our fancy,
We buy them "*Brums*," "*Caleys*," or "*Apes.*"
Dear "*Bertha*" I have not forgotten,
She's really a feature in "*Rails;*"
And tho' some of my tips have been rotten,
I landed some money in "*Mails.*"
"*Potts*," "*Berwicks*," and "*Bags*" I am buying,
And "*Rollers*" and "*Vestas*" I hold;
Where's the use of eternally crying?
Some day we shall strike on the gold.

* * * * *

Oh! supposing our "*Cream jugs*" were broken,
Or "*Beetles*" were scaring the "*Babies*,"
While our "*Guns*" were in soak in the "*Milk Cans*,
And the "*Dogs*" had run wild with the rabies.

HOUSE SCRAPS.

What with "*Cables*" and with "*Wires*,"
When anything transpires
To send the market either up or down;
    In aërated "*Breads*,"
    Or "*Shores*," or "*Yanks*," or "*Reds*,"
In slang we really do it rather brown;
    But when the members fail,
    Why, then the dealers quail,
For it sets the "*Hammer*" working up and down.

THE EXECUTION; OR, HAMMERED.

A. B. C. FOR THE STOCK EXCHANGE.

BY F. C. GOULD. *Published in 1875.*

Unfortunately, the caricatures which were published with the book are not to be had, the plates having been destroyed.

A
Stands for Angle,
  So fierce and so bold,
Whose boxing, they say,
  Is a sight to behold.

B
's Braggiotti,
  An "Irredenta;"
All the English he knows is
  "You full! Ah doon kar."

C
Stands for the Cohens,
  Alfred and Benny,
Nat, Lionel, Louis,
  The "Dutch Mail" and Lenny.

D
Is for Downer,
  Who, the multitude shouts,
Columbus surpassed
  By discovering Sprouts.

E
Is for Ellissen,
  Who, people say,
Is on the piano
  Well able to play.

F
Is for Fanty,
  Who jobs all the day,
And piles up the cash
  When Castello's away.

G
Stands for Goldschmidt,
  When not up to his larks,
He's always croaking
  And screeching for Ma-arx.

H
Is for Hamilton,
  Who aiblins have thocht,
That mirover she will
  Hef peen ta'en for a Scot.

I
Is for W. T. F. M. Ingall
  He's often resigned;
But is not meek at all.

J
Is for Joseph,
  Who, though slightly obese,
Has been seen at the Argyll
  By the police.

K
Is McKenna,
  K's the first letther, shure!
Mc only manes
  He's an Oirishman pure.

L
Is for Lodge,
  Who smole, so they say,
When he saw a poor infant
  Run over one day.

M
Is the Monk
  We so often attack,
By suggestions that ducks
  Are accustomed to quack!

N
Is Tom Nickalls;
  He's equally frantic,
Whether hunting a stag,
  Or banging "Atlantic.

O
Is for Oliver,
  Who into a flurry,
  Remorselessly teases
  Poor Downer and Murray.

P
Stands for Pyemont,
  Who once, it is said,
  Spent four days and nights
  Reflecting in bed.

Q
For Quihampton,
  Who, no doubt, has a pup
  Which he'll enter this year
  For the Waterloo Cup.

R
Is for Richardson,
  Murray, I mean,
  He's as vigorous now
  As ever he's been.

S
For Selous,
  Whose genius dramatic
  Made his "True to the Core"
  A success most emphatic.

T
Stands for Trew—
  Between me and you,
  When he's been hunting
  He gets in a sad stew.

U
Is for Underhill—
  He's supposed to be nice,
  But on the committee
  He's distinguished as "Vice."

V
Is for Vardon—
  Though he looks so austere,
  'Tis said that he really
  Is not so severe.

W
's Wilkinson,
  The elegant Tarral,
  He looks quite the thing
  In his hunting apparel.

X
Whenever there's larking
  One always expects
  To find its some nonsense
  Of Mr. Gus Eck's.

Y
Is Y. Williams—
  Why Williams is why,
  You must ask that of some one
  Who's wiser than I.

Z
Zalig's the last,
  And Zalig's the least;
  Thus endeth the lesson,
  Enough is a feast.

BEAR AND BULL-BAITING IN THE NEW WORLD.

Fisk, the New York market-rigger, whose wonderful fiscal performances have lately held him up to the admiration of Europe as the most colossal of operators and the biggest of all bulls—a veritable Bull of Bashan—started in life, we are told, as a circus-rider. This may help to account for his daring feats in the ring, and his power of keeping up his balance under difficulties. . . . . But how strange it is to see the sports of the bear-bait and the bull-ring, which the Old World has put down as degrading and brutal, revived on this gigantic scale in the New.—*Punch*, November 6th, 1869.

MUCH ADO ABOUT NOTHING IN THE CITY.

Sigh no more, dealers, sigh no more,
  Shares were unstable ever,
They often have been down before,
  At high rates constant never.

Then sigh not so,
Soon up they'll go,
  And you'll be blithe and funny,
Converting all your notes of woe,
  Into hey, money, money.

Write no more letters, write no mo'
  On stocks so dull and heavy;
At times on 'Change 'tis always so,
  When bears a tribute levy.

Then sigh not so,
And don't be low,
  In sunshine you'll make honey,
Converting all your notes of woe,
  Into hey, money, money.

Punch, September 28th, 1867.

LOOK BEFORE YOU LEND.

(Song for the Stock Exchange.)

If you invest in foreign funds, brave boys, let cash be lent
With sole regard to int'rest—not per sentiment, per cent.
The man who talks of moral wrong, upholding tyrant rule,
Aiding aggression, robbery, war, and bloodshed, is a fool.

No matter if you should suspect, or even if you know,
You're laying out your capital to help a foreign foe
With ironclads and monster guns. Ne'er stick to lend him aid;
Care not but for the assurance that you'll get your interest paid.

But oh, make very sure of that, and keep a weather eye
To the use for which your Despot wants the funds which you supply.
You can't be too particular, if all he gets he spends
As well upon unrighteous as unprofitable ends.

In venturing an investment that will serve immoral ends,
Mind you've a borrower capable of cheating him who lends,
Whence, mourning love of lucre, too confiding City gents
Wish they had been contented with their native Three-per-Cents.

Punch, July 1st, 1876.

A CURIOSITY.

This curious business card is well worth re-producing. I think it is about 100 years old. Mr. Morgan Vaughan was never a member of the present Stock Exchange.

All the members in 1801 were compelled to abandon any other business if they wanted to remain in the House. Perhaps Mr. Vaughan preferred to remain an "outsider."

THE BANKING REFORM NEEDED.

To substitute the (comparatively) limited lie-ability of shareholders, for the positively unlimited lie-ability of directors (*vide* Glasgow Bank revelations).—*Punch*, 22nd February, 1879.

BROKERS AND JOKERS.

Says the *Globe* (December 26th), in an article on "Sworn Brokers:"— "Brokers there are, alas! but not sworn brokers." Now we have met with brokers who have sworn, and we have encountered brokers who have been sworn at, and we have known brokers who have "sworn off." Surely these should compensate for the loss of the "sworn broker," whom, we are informed, no longer exists.—*Punch*, January 5th, 1884.

FISHING IN SCOTLAND.

A young member once opened a large account for the rise, and then suddenly disappeared. On the contango day, as he was not to be found, the jobbers having accounts with him closed them; the stocks had risen considerably, therefore large differences were due to him.

A week or two after the account he coolly returned to the House, and claimed the sums due to him. On being asked where he had been, he said, " fishing in Scotland."

"And suppose," said a member, "we had had a big fall and you had lost your money, where would you be now?"

"Still fishing in Scotland," replied the cool one.

SONG OF A SHAREHOLDER.

Collisions, when they railway trains befall,
    Increase the weight of my domestic cares,
Because, indeed, I have my little all
    Invested, most of it in railway shares.

When bones are broken and when lives are lost,
    We suffer with the victims and their friends;
They are bereaved or injured at our cost,
    Their damages reduce our dividends.

This is the question:—were't the better way
    On dear precautions money to expend?
Or frequent compensation have to pay?
    Which policy were cheaper in the end?

This doubt it now behoves us to decide,
    For if unsettled it much longer stands,
Rulers, for public safety to provide,
    Might take our business out of private hands.

The telegraphs they took to the sole end
    Of cheap despatch; still stronger is the plea,
Which, for the like assumption, may commend
    Mismanaged railways to the powers that be.

If we, for parsimony's doubtful gains,
    Risk our investment of productive store,
Then, to prevent the clash of crowded trains,
    Had we not better lay out rather more?

Punch, September 26th, 1874.

STOCK EXCHANGE REFORM.

Restore the parochial stocks and also the pillory, put the greater rogues amongst the stock-speculators, riggers, ringers, promoters, and bubble-blowers into the one, and the lesser—if there be any—in the other.—*Punch*, March 31st, 1877.

DIRECTORS' QUALIFICATIONS.

It is proposed to institute Competitive Examinations of persons desirous of becoming Directors, Secretaries, or Promoters of Public Companies. Specimen Papers:—

EXAMINATION PAPER FOR DIRECTORS.

1. What is your qualification for the post? Have you been (*a*) a member of the Government of British Timbuctoo; (*b*) the Parliamentary Representative of the Free and Independent Electors of Bribeborough; or (*c*) a Managing Director of the Herne Bay, American and Spanish Credit Financier Company?

2. Do you know anything of the business of the Company of which you desire to become a Director? If you are forced to answer this question in the affirmative, state any extenuating circumstances that may occur to you.

3. Give your method for examining the books of a Company without looking at the items or testing the totals.

4. Explain the theory of "how not to do it," and give a table of what you consider reasonable Directors' Fees.

5. How many "qualifying shares" will you require in return for your name and in payment of your trouble?

EXAMINATION PAPER FOR SECRETARIES.

1. How many " Names" can you add to a list of Directors?

2. Can you undertake that your nominees shall give no trouble at the meetings of the Board?

3. Do you thoroughly understand Financial Cookery in all its branches?

4. Do you know how to dress up a Minute Book?

5. How much do you charge per annum for holding your tongue and shutting your eyes?

EXAMINATION PAPER FOR PROMOTERS.

1. How many times have you been a Bankrupt?

2. Do you thoroughly understand the various methods of evading payment of a County Court summons?

3. Show to the satisfaction of the Examiners that 2 and 3 amount to 27.

4. Write out Prospectuses for the following imaginary Companies, proving them all to be the most lucrative investments that have ever been submitted to an intelligent public—

    (*a*) The Goodwin Sands Railway Company;
    (*b*) The North Pole Wine Manufacturing Company;
    (*c*) The Swiss Sea-Salt Company;
    (*d*) The Moon and Stars Diamond Fields Company.

5. State (*a*) the countries under extradition treaties with England; (*b*) the offences cognisable under such treaties respectively; and (*c*) given a financial emergency, describe on the map the most expeditious and secret route to Spain.—*Punch*, February 27th, 1875.

SIR MOSES MONTEFIORE.

DIED, JULY 28TH, 1885, IN HIS HUNDRED-AND-FIRST YEAR.

Is life worth living? To the querulous cry
Let this long record, lately closed, reply!
A century of service to mankind!
Pessimist cold, and cynic blandly blind,
'Tis fitter comment on that query stale
Than sneers that pall and arguments that fail.
Long in the land his days, whose heart and hand
All high and human causes could command;
Long in the land his memory will abide,
His country's treasure and his people's pride.

Punch, August 8th, 1885.

THE CROAK OF THE CAPITALIST.

I heard a man of money, which he wanted to invest,
A melancholy *millionaire*, unload his anxious breast.
Meanwhile he scanned and scrutinized a list of shares and stocks:
The banks and mines and shipping lines, the railways and the docks.

" Tell me of Statesmen's private and pecuniary affairs;
Say in which Joint Stock Companies the chief of them hold shares;
What published list of shareholders, oh! where can I obtain,
That I may by example go the safest way to gain?

" Those Government securities should be the most secure
Which governing financiers show that they themselves count sure—
For Downing Street is downy, and in general wideawake,
Though sometimes in a Budget there is made a slight mistake.

" However, touching some that take the Communistic view,
While to the many they propose to sacrifice the few,
But confiscation still to 'scape undoubtedly design;
What care they take of their own wealth, I too might take of mine."

Punch, January 17th, 1885.

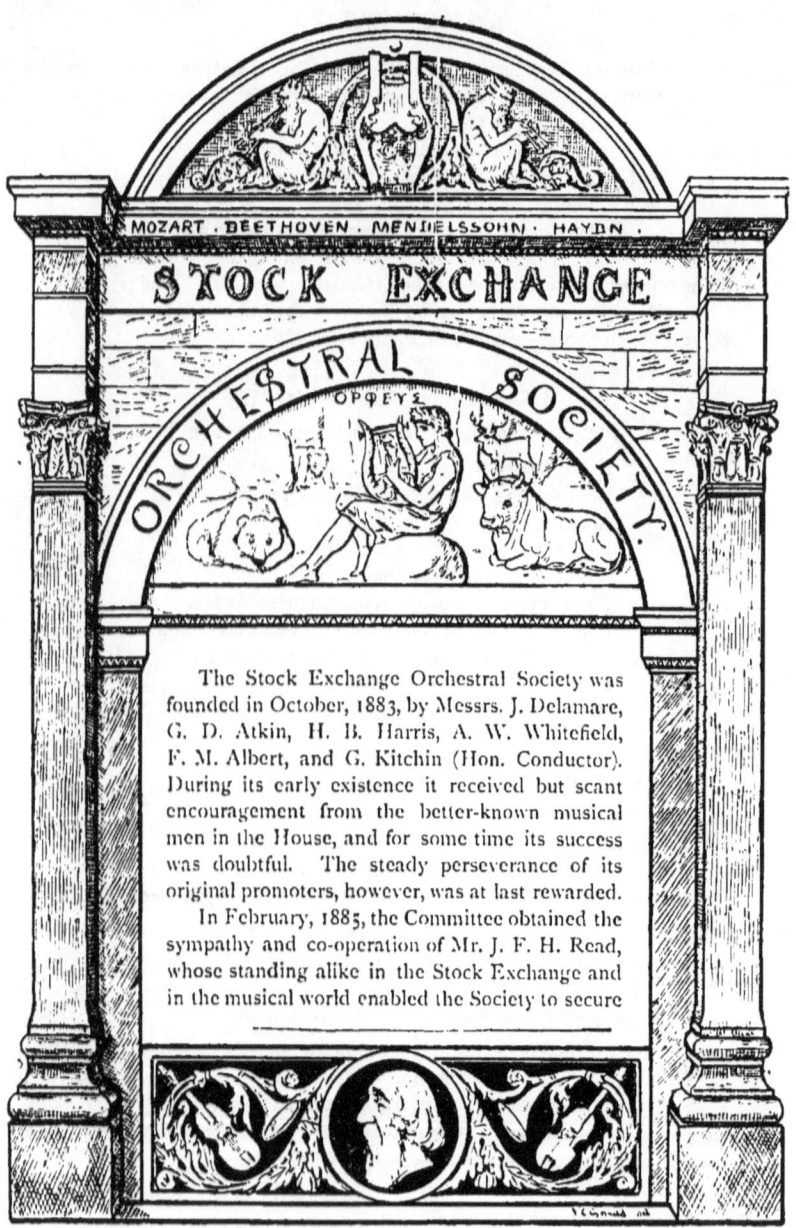

MOZART . BEETHOVEN . MENDELSSOHN . HAYDN .

STOCK EXCHANGE
ORCHESTRAL SOCIETY.
ΟΡΦΕΥΣ

The Stock Exchange Orchestral Society was founded in October, 1883, by Messrs. J. Delamare, G. D. Atkin, H. B. Harris, A. W. Whitefield, F. M. Albert, and G. Kitchin (Hon. Conductor). During its early existence it received but scant encouragement from the better-known musical men in the House, and for some time its success was doubtful. The steady perseverance of its original promoters, however, was at last rewarded.

In February, 1885, the Committee obtained the sympathy and co-operation of Mr. J. F. H. Read, whose standing alike in the Stock Exchange and in the musical world enabled the Society to secure the support necessary to its continuation. A concert, given in the St. Andrew's Hall in aid of the Clerks' Provident Fund, convinced those who were holding aloof that ample material existed in the House for the formation of an efficient orchestra. Since then, two successful series of concerts have been given in Prince's Hall: and the Society now numbers about fifty-five active and one hundred and fifty honorary members.

THE SIGH OF THE STOCK BROKER.

(BUSINESS IS VERY DULL ON THE STOCK EXCHANGE.)

It was a weary stock broker who stood in Capel Court—
That's just outside the Stock Exchange, where brokers most resort;
Quoth he, " In speculation there's a most disastrous lull,
And business in the City is indubitably dull.

" There's nothing doing in the House in any stocks or shares,
And very silent are the ' Bulls,' and angry are the ' Bears ;'
'Tis no use dealing with ourselves, endeavouring to 'best'
Each other, when the public won't be tempted to invest.

" I've tried my hand at Mexicans, and sold them in a funk;
And often I've been in and out of Canada's Grand Trunk;
I've dabbled in Egyptians,—you don't catch me there again ;—
I've lost in rails American, and burnt my hands with Spain.

" It's no good going on like this, for all men know, I ween,
The proverb says it's bad for crows to ' pick out corbies' een ;'
We prey upon each other, since the public shows no flats,
And very soon must emulate the famed Kilkenny cats."

So moaned that poor young stock broker in accents sad and sour,
He scarce could cock his glossy hat, he sported ne'er a flower;
And as he wandered West upon his melancholy way,
He hadn't tasted dry champagne through all the weary day.

Philanthropists of England, ye who go to the Lord Mayor,
And ask him to get up new funds, presiding in the chair,
Now surely in the Mansion House a meeting ye should hold,
To give the hapless stock broker once more a glimpse of gold.

Punch, November 3rd, 1883.

THE MONEY MARKET.

Cash was rather shy, and lenders particularly bashful; while the demands for loans were brisk, and the refusals flatter than usual. Promissory scrip commanded nothing; and on settling day berths in the Boulogne steam-boats rose to a very high and unhealthy premium. Bills were not in request, but the acceptors of some that were overdue were a good deal sought after. A party with money made his appearance in the afternoon, and a stranger, having completed a rapid transfer of the funds, took the turn of the market, and withdrew immediately.—*Punch*, 1842.

a good long

a heavy fall

a good puff

FEELING OF THE CITY.

(AMONGST BULLS AND BEARS.)

Russian 1870. Rising market. "Let the two barbarians fight it out, sir! What have *we* to do with it?"

Hungarian 1871. Heavy fall. "We must take care that other countries don't interfere. General war!—horrible!"

Italian 1861. Slight fall. "I should like to know what *they* have to do with it? Gross impudence!"

French Threes. Steady. "Of course France will be neutral. Hope there'll be no more talk of annexing Egypt."

Portuguese Threes. Unsteady. "Too bad! Lord Beaconsfield is playing the very mischief with business!"

Turkish Fives. Slight rise. "Plucky fellows, sir; and if old Pam were alive we should have gone in for 'em long before this."

Austrian Silver Rentes. Heavy, with a downward tendency. "Only want a spirited policy to pull us through. Always thought the Triple Alliance bosh!"

Spanish Actives. Very dead. "After all, if there is a general war, what matter its horrors, if our honour demands it?"

Argentine Sixes. Heavy, and going down. "Mere madness to think of fighting! What is prestige compared with prices?"

Russian Fives. Rising. "The Turks should be forced to conclude peace, sir. Forced, sir! forced!"

Turkish Fives. No demand. "It is simply suicidal to think of a Turkish Alliance. Russia is our best friend, and always has been."

Egypt Preference. Falling. "We ought to declare war against Russia immediately, and occupy Egypt. British interests demand this step, sir. The sooner the better!"—*Punch*, January 26th, 1878.

PROSPECTUS FOR A PROVIDENT ANNUITY COMPANY.

1. The Capital of this Company is to consist of £0,000,001; one-half of it to be vested in Aldgate Pump, and the other moiety in the Dogger Bank.

2. Shares at £50 each, will be issued to any amount, and interest paid thereon when convenient.

3. A board, consisting of twelve Directors, will be formed; but, to save trouble, the management of the Company's affairs will be placed in the hands of the Secretary.

4. The duties of Trustees, Auditor, and Treasurer, will also be discharged by the Secretary.

5. Each Shareholder will be presented with a gratuitous copy of the Company's regulations, printed on fine foolscap.

6. Individuals purchasing annuities of this Company will be allowed a large rate of interest, on paper, for their money, calculated on an entirely novel sliding scale. Annuitants will be entitled to receive their annuities whenever they can get them.

7. The Company's office will be open at all hours for the receipt of money; but it is not yet determined at what time the paying branch of the department will come into operation.

8. The Secretary will be allowed the small salary of £10,000 a year.

9. In order to simplify the accounts, there will be no books kept. By this arrangement a large saving will be effected in the article of clerks, etc.

10. The annual profits of the Company will be fixed at 20 per cent., but it is expected that there will be no enquiry made after dividends.

11. All monies received for and by the Company to be deposited in the breeches-pocket of the Secretary, and not to be withdrawn from thence without his special sanction.

12. The establishment to consist of a Secretary and Porter.

13. The Porter is empowered to act as Secretary in the absence of that officer, and the Secretary is permitted to assist the Porter in the arduous duties of his situation.

* Applications for shares or annuities to be made to the Secretary of the Provident Annuity Company, No. 1, Thieves' Inn.

Punch, 28th, 1841.

———

Gold was in a feverish state owing to the process of sweating, and parties who expected to find money extremely heavy were surprised at its uncommon lightness, which they only perceived when bringing it into the market. Sovereigns, with the coupons (or little pieces) cut out, were freely offered for twenty shillings and as freely declined, and many persons made fruitless endeavours to turn the scale by filling in the crevices.

Punch, 1842.

A CITY CIRCULAR.

(Picked up near to Capel Court.)

Messrs. Bunkum, Jingo & Co., according to their custom, beg to present their clients with their opinion upon affairs in general, and the foreign policy of the Government in particular.

The money market is much disturbed, thus offering an excellent opportunity to investors to operate to advantage. Enclosed in the wrapper containing this paper will be found a list of excellent securities.

Messrs. Bunkum, Jingo & Co., particularly recommend the shares of the Mexican and Dismal Swamp Junction Railway Company, the Bank of England North Pole Gold Mines, and the Herne Bay Residential Club and Champagne and Coffee Palace Chambers. All these investments are now at an unprecedented low price, and must ultimately yield large returns, &c., &c.—*Punch*, June 7th, 1884.

ONE OF NAPOLEON'S OLD GUARD DETAILING AT SOME LENGTH HIS LAST TRIP TO THE ENGADINE.—*April, 1876.*

Cash was excessively loose on Christmas-day; but it became much tighter on the demand for Christmas-boxes. The Waterloo Bridge new debentures, with the dividend of two-pence, payable on or before the 25th March, 1873, are heavy at nothing; while the dividend itself is so buoyant, that in spite of the eagerness to realise no one was found to have a hand in it.— 1843.

THE HOUSE THAT COLE BUILT.

This is the house that Cole built.

These are the managers stern and grand,
Who hold their sway with an iron hand,
   And who dwell in the house that Cole built.

And these are the jobbers, blithe and gay,
Who job and play in their pleasing way,
And are ruled by the managers, stern and grand
Who hold their sway with an iron hand,
   And who dwell in the house that Cole built.

And these are the brokers, who, day by day,
Deal with the jobbers, blithe and gay,
Who job and play in their pleasing way,
And are ruled by the managers, stern and grand,
Who hold their sway with an iron hand,
   And who dwell in the house that Cole built.

And this is the Como, a source of gain,
Which lightens sorrow and eases pain,
And cheers the brokers, who, day by day,
Deal with the jobbers, blithe and gay,
Who job and play in their pleasing way,
And are ruled by the managers, stern and grand,
Who hold their sway with an iron hand,
   And who dwell in the house that Cole built.

And these are the clients who sell and buy,
Who "bear" when low, and "bull" when high,
And who pay the Como, a source of gain,
Which lightens sorrow and eases pain,
And cheers the brokers, who, day by day,
Deal with the jobbers, blithe and gay,
Who job and play in their pleasing way,
And are ruled by the managers, stern and grand,
Who hold their sway with an iron hand,
   And who dwell in the house that Cole built.

And these are the men who, all forlorn,
Wander about all tattered and torn,
Who have been clients, who sell and buy,
Who "bear" when low, and "bull" when high,

THE ARCHITECT OF THE TEMPLE OF THE BULL AND BEAR.

And who pay the Como, a source of gain,
Which lightens sorrow and eases pain,
And cheers the brokers, who, day by day,
Deal with the jobbers, blithe and gay,
Who job and play in their pleasing way,
And are ruled by the managers, stern and grand,
Who hold their sway with an iron hand,
    And who dwell in the house that Cole built.

A NEWS PROVIDER.

Mr. Samuel Crisp, who died about the year 1784, was a stock broker, and retired from business with an easy competency. His daily amusement, for the last fourteen years of his life, was throwing into the letter-box of the several newspapers slips of paper containing short hints and broken sentences; and to gather materials for these he travelled in the stage from London to Greenwich, and back again, in the same coach every day. The owner of the Greenwich stage, never anticipating that he would have so constant a customer, had agreed to carry him at all times for £27 a year, but he refused at last to stand by his agreement, and this, with some other mortifications from the newspaper editors, who did not value his favours at quite so high a rate as he thought they merited, put an end to poor Mr. Crisp's life.—*Percy Anecdotes.*

THE STOCK JOBBER'S LAMENT.

[The following poem, by Horace Smith, (of whom there is a notice in another part of this book), was published in 1813 in a book of poems entitled, " Horace in London: by Horace and James Smith."]

 O fatal Omnium, wicked was his noddle
  Who first created (omen of ill luck)
 Thee, doomed to make thy holder almost waddle,
  And turn a green goose to a limping duck.

 Napoleon, who with me has play'd the devil,
  Has doubtless acted it with many more;
 In midnight massacres disposed to revel,
  Or poison soldiers upon Jaffa's shore.

 All other crimes I could forgive thee, Boney,
  But this exceeds the blackest in degree;
 'Tis murderous sacrilege to take my money,
  For money is both life and soul to me.

 We cannot all of us be always winners—
  Bulls will hold on when markets mock their art;
 And disappointed Bears, tho' cunning sinners,
  Sometimes hold off when prices upward shoot.

 Fortune takes one behind her on a pillion;
  Another, whom to-day she tumbles down,
 To-morrow she may bless with half-a-million,
  And leave the first with scarcely half-a-crown.

 How narrow my escape from utter ruin!
  On the black-board I thought to see my name,
 Where every sneering brother Bull or Bruin,
  Might read at once my losses and my shame.

There future Ducks, who in hot water dabble,
    Chatter of leagues and wars in sounds confused;
Others of Long Annuities will gabble,
    Or prate of my Appropriate Fund—Reduced.

But what a sudden truce to their debating
    When the commissioners are served with stock!
Then Bulls and Bears, no more each other baiting,
    Round a new pivot clamorously flock.

Three-headed Cerberus stands mute with wonder
    To find his roar excelled by human tongue,
With lifted hands all bellowing like thunder—
    A fleet of fingers in a storm of lungs.

Rise from the shades, old Orpheus, with thy fiddle,
    To quell the row among the biped cattle;
Bid Bulls with dancing Bears lead down the middle,
    So shall their tongues and heels in concert rattle.

THE STOCK EXCHANGE ALPHABET.

A is our Architect, weighed with care.
B stands for Broker, for Bull, and for Bear.
C 's the Contango that's paid by the Bull.
D the Defaulter who can't pay in full.
E the Electric Light—always going out.
F the Financiers, who're never in doubt.
G for the cheese—Gorgonzola by name.
H for the House that is built of the same.
I the Investor, with good store of cash.
J is the jobber, who cuts such a dash.
K are the knowing ones—awfully clever.
L is the Limit, which cometh off never.
M are the Managers, stern, yet serene.
N are the Notice boards everywhere seen.
O is the Option to put or to call.
P is the Panic that causes a fall.
Q 's the Quotation the brokers require.
R are the Rates which rise higher and higher.
S Speculator, who stumbles along.
T is the "good Tip"—invariably wrong!
U is the stock which we Unified call.
V the Valarium which hangs over all.
W for Wetenhall, famed for his list.
X is a letter I fear must be missed.
Y are the Yankees whose prices we get.
Z is the Zeal this is done with—you bet!

Certain Tips.—Something that is sure to rise during the next three months—the thermometer. Something that is sure to fall—rain.

MR. DAVID WILKINSON PLAYS THE "DICKENS" WITH THE "CHRISTMAS CAROL."
Epsom, 13th January, 1875.

THE MONEY MARKET.

Our own funds have not improved since our last, and property of a certain description has gone up (the spout) in consequence. Our watch is now quoted at 15s. with the coupon, which carries interest at 3d. per month; and French stock was done, without the stiffener, at one-and-nine-pence.

  *   *   *   *   *

Foreign funds are remarkably good, which partly accounts for our enormous circulation. There were no Consols in the market, though it was reported that there was one at Boulogne. In shares, Grand Junctions were at a discount, owing to the great scarcity of buttons.

1842.

Transfer of stocks may be effected at any respectable cravat-sellers on any particular day except Sunday, which is kept as a holiday. A power of attorney is not necessary, although it is often out of the power of attorney's clerks to get a new *stock*. The transfer is generally made by the payment of a certain sum and leaving the old one behind to be recovered, or because it is not worth taking away.

Punch Almanack, 1843.

THE CAPEL COURT DOORKEEPER ON CHRISTMAS-BOXES.

(SPECIALLY COMMUNICATED.)

Crismus only kums once a year, and not always just then, i spose, in leap year, though i've never kep' my eye on it pertickler; but i think as some o' the gents in the 'Ouse wishes as 'ow it could be left out sometimes, as they ain't all as flush o' money as people might think, becoz I nose difrent, being edgeoocated up to 'em. I don't mind lettin' you into a secret, coz I bleeve you'll keep my identity wailed, an' I've disgised my andriting, though that ain't praps much pertection after its wonst printed, wich is, that *'taint always klients and clarks as asks for a name to be cauled.'* I've seen men s'piciously like bootmakers an' such, with letters 'avin' "wait for an arnser" wrote on 'em, an' more thern twice, i've seen a party with a buttond-up koat, an' smelling o' rits, waiting about some hours or more.

I could tell some kurious things if only i was so disposed, wich i ain't. Secrets with hus is all a matter o' pounds, shillings and pence, an' not too much of the pence, an' if we're tipped propper, nothing never passes our lips, but wot the gents intended, meaning beer. I've never said nothing about none on 'em as didn't forget me; an' them as did, why i've treted 'em as beneath me, which they are. Besides, yer see, a still tung shows a Y. Z., and not only that, but yer keep yer place longer. A Stock Exchange waiter ain't arrived at without some inconvenyence, and yer 'as ter speak up for it to; if you carn't friten a sparrer orf a 'ouse-top by just openin' yer mouth, yer ain't no good for a doorkeeper. We livs by our voices, jest the same as Adderleaner Patty or a orkshuneer, and we're lookd up to by all them clarks and such-like as we orders ware to stand, and don't 'urry to call out the memmbers as they wants; hand they 'as to be preshus civvil to, or we keaps 'em waitin', like the pleece do the omlibusses. I nevr could stand the bounce them clarks puts on; blo' me, if yer woudn't think as some of 'em wern't doorkeepers themselves bi the hairs they assoom, an' wot with their kollars an' their 'ats, an' their siggerets, an' the 'urry they're always in, they sets my bak up. But I'm the ed of the Kapel Court lobby, an' them as don't like it can go to *sum hother dor.*

The Capel Court dor is the most gentlmanly dor o' the lot, orl the best brokers use it, an' the jobbers as comes threw deal in Konsols, and the 'Ouse shairs, an' the funds, an' nun of yer forrin or mining muck. We're orful select at that dor, an' its very seldom as we 'as eny of the Noo Cort lofers 'anging about *hus*, an' a good job i ses, for it lowers yer in yer own estimashun to 'ave to keap on corling out the gents for them chaps. But round at the mining dor's the werst for that kind of thing: i've bean puffectly serprized to sea some o' them outside mining delers akshally a-doing biznis *inside* the swing-dors. I'd nevr allow it in mi loby, not for nothing, an' not eaven if they giv' me 'arf a krown each time, wich they coodn't run too. But dores soon make a difrence, an' i've noan a fellow-gentlman, who's allways kep' 'imself moast select at Kapel Cort, get scent to the mining door, an' then I've seen 'im demeening 'imself by larfin' with a kerbstone deler in a fortnight. As for me, I make a praktis of looking' strait in frunt wen anywun as I considers beneath me arsks me a question; an' altho' i arnsers 'em, as in dooty bound, I makes 'em as short an' disagrebl as possible. Mind, i ain't a snob: I utterly refute that idear. I don't judge bi the koat he wares, or the joolery, or nothing of that kind; no, i judges 'im by 'is hair, and if 'e speeks gentlemanly, i speeks gentlemanly to, pervidin' 'e ain't ackshally in raggs.

But its about Krismus as i was more particklerly going too rite, sinse a gentleman from yor offis come and tempt me, in a way I couldn't resist, so to do; and he sez, "If you can drop in anything pussonal, so much the better." To wich I replys, with that dignety for wich i'm so konspikyewus, "Sir," I sez, "I never sez nothing pussonal, becoz it ain't gentlemanly; an', wot's more, it may get me in a row." But as i've promist to say a little bit about the Crismus-boxes I get from the gents in the 'Ouse, w'y i'll do it.

In the ferst plaice, then, it don't kum to so much as some might think for; an' if yer arsk me my pryvate opinyun, I think the hoppersite sex seas more o' their money than is good for 'em. The gents as keeps their kotes a 'anging about me all day, an' whom i ain't abuv 'elpin on with 'em, of course they 'as to giv' me sumthing, an' they duz it, an' there's an end of it. But some of the other gents from 'oom I mite go so far as to say i expex something, in konseqwens of little od jobs in the way of letters and such-like, i *will* say they don't allways cum up to my expektashuns. It ain't in me to tel 'em so; i'd sooner beg my bred elsewear than arsk for a penny; thow bekaws my weakness is extream reserve, it ain't for them to take advantige of it. But I doan't wish to make a noospaper the vehikkle of my private rongs, an' sew i'll drop 'em. Them as may read this wil no whoom i mene; and if the kap fits 'em, they'll no they've brort it on their own 'eds.

I've made sum rarther wawm remarks about clarks, but i wish moast emfatically to say that i don't inclood the gents they corls markit clarks among 'em. These, as a rool, is most generus at Crismus-time; weather it is that they think they've got to show the waiters they're as good as the propper members, or weather it is 'coz they givs away other pepl's money, I don't no; but I do know that they givs it, an' wot's maw, I nose that i takes it. Nex' to them, kums them gentlemen as 'as gells to meat 'em sumtimes, and who ar verry censitiv to 'aving a propper respectful bareing shoan to 'em, espeshly wen, as *'as* 'appened, a yung lady 'as walked up to the very dore an' arst me to korl Mr. So-an'-so. Lor', 'ow them chaps do blush w'en they kums out unexpekted like that, an' seas all the gentlemen that passes a-larfin'! I never larfs then, as it pays me best not to, but i won't say that i don't indullge in a sollum wink w'en the gent's bak is turnd. But that's only yewman naitcher.

But them gentlemen as dreses themselves up so as you don't no wich is them, an' wich is their close, are the ones to walk parst without seaing yer at Crismus-time. Wot it must kossed them to keep levole with the tailors' shops in the way they doo is apauling to think ov, and no wonder that they kuts their lunches down, and tries to dodg us out of our doos! But I never takes no mor noatice than a contemptuous snear, an' wood scorn to remind 'em by any seizenable remarks, like sum of my fellow-waiters ain't abuv doing. I nose they'll get punished for it some time or other by going out with there 'at ruff'd, or a slip of paper stuk on their bax, or something of that spesees, of which I should tell 'em if they'd only shoan me ordinary fealing. One of this sort wonce sez to me at Crismus-time, 'olding a 'arf-crown in 'is 'and, " Peace on earth, John, an' goodwil tords men. You've got my goodwill, but i'll keap the *peace* miself," an' 'e poets it bak in 'is pokit, an' larfs. An' the verry nex' day he'd rub'd himself against sumthing, an' got a wite mark on 'is bak! D' yer think i rub'd it orf? no.

The Trunk markit's the most lib'ral, but i don't sea much of *them*. Mr. Tom ——, well p'rhaps i'd better not menshun names, tho' 'e is the most open-handed gen'l'man as ever i see, an' so's Mr. 'arry ——, but the same reezun stops my mowth. Both of 'em belong to it. There's a few fussy 'orty gents as yewses mi dor who gives me a 'arf-krown at Crismus as tho' they expekted me to go down on my neas w'enever i seize 'em for it, but not mee. I don't say as i woodn't do it in sperrit if they giv' me enuff, but i ain't agoing to abase miself for nuthing pawltry.

On the 'ole, I ain't got much komplaynt against most o' the gents. I've sean better, an' I've seane werse; I takes 'em as they kums, an' if they don't tip me why they *don't*, an' there's no luv lossed between us.

Money, December 22nd, 1886.

THE ASS AND THE THISTLE.

A wise man laugh'd to see an ass
Eat thistles and neglect good grass;
But had the sage beheld the folly
Of late transacted in 'Change Alley,
He might have seen worse asses there
Give solid gold for empty air,
And sell estates, in hopes to double
Their fortunes, by some worthless Bubble.
Till of a sudden all was lost,
That had so many millions cost;
Yet ruin'd fools are highly pleas'd,
To see the knaves that bit 'em squeez'd,
Forgetting where the money flies,
That costs so many tears and sighs.

A STRANGE DISCOVERY IN THE CIT-TEE DESERT.

THE STOCK EXCHANGE.

I sing the song of the Stock Exchange!
    In the days of *Pyemont* the King,
"Stag-hunting *Tom*," and "*Clem Satterthwaite*,"
    And the boys of the Erie Ring!

There are some of the lads of Teutonic race,
    Who come from the Fatherland;
And *Sydney Claris*, and *J. P. Trew*,
    Who driveth a four-in-hand!

The Pug of the house, and the *Medley Crew*,
    Who deal in the Yankee Things;
Old *Nettleton* and a heap of Clerks,
    And the *Clarke* who whistles and sings.

HOUSE SCRAPS. 95

There's another *Clark* who deals in Banks,
  The Waterworks and the Docks;
Then *Prance*, and *Wedd*, and *Marshall Paine*,
  For the Trunks and Canadian Stocks.

In the Foreign market you'll find the spot,
  Where the *Bakers* make their bread.
John Heseltine, and the *Cohen* lot,
  Near the ancient *Lobb* and *Wedd*.

In the English market before the Bar,
  The *Prices* and the *Bones*,
Mitchell and old *Bill Ekyn* are,
  And *Brown* and *Smith* and *Jones*.

Old *Moore* above the mining world,
  Smiles grimly on the scene;
While *Avory* and the others play,
  As boys play on the green.

a. wide margin.

Oh oh! ha ha! the mining world,
  And the men who deal in mines ;
And Electric Shocks and Peruvian Stocks,
  And all the Railway lines.

Then glory to the Thirty-four,
  And to the gallant Ten,
Who, led by *Scott* and *Underhill*,
  Control these merry men.

And when the next Election comes,
  Still may they hold their own;
And may their Secretaries be,
  Levien and *Will Perowne*.'

A SOUTH-SEA BALLAD.

In London stands a famous pile,
  And near that pile an alley,
Where merry crowds for riches toil,
  And wisdom stoops to folly.
Here sad and joyful, high and low,
  Court fortune for her graces,
And as she smiles, or frowns, they show,
  Their gestures and grimaces.

Here stars and garters do appear,
  Among our lords the rabble,
To buy and sell, to see and hear
  The Jews and Gentiles squabble.

Here crafty courtiers are too wise
    For those who trust to fortune;
They see the cheat with clearer eyes,
    Who peep behind the curtain.

Our greatest ladies hither come,
    And ply in chariots daily;
Oft pawn their jewels for a sum,
    To venture 't in the alley.
Young harlots, too, from Drury Lane,
    Approach the 'Change in coaches,
To fool away the gold they gain
    By their obscene debauches.

Long heads may thrive by sober rules,
    Because they think and drink not,
But headlongs are our thriving fools,
    Who only drink and think not.
The lucky rogues, like spaniel dogs,
    Leap into South-Sea water,
And there they fish for golden frogs,
    Not caring what comes a'ter.

'Tis said that alchymists of old
    Could turn a brazen kettle,
Or leaden cistern, into gold—
    That noble, tempting metal;
But if it here may be allow'd
    To bring in great with small things,
Our cunning South-Sea, like a god,
    Turns nothing into all things.

What need have we of Indian wealth,
    Or commerce with our neighbours;
Our constitution is in health,
    And riches crown our labours.
Our South-Sea ships have golden shrouds,
    They bring us wealth, 'tis granted,
But lodge their treasure in the clouds,
    To hide it till it's wanted.

O Britain! bless thy present state,
    Thou only happy nation,
So oddly rich, so madly great,
    Since Bubbles came in fashion.
Successful rakes exert their pride,
    And count their airy millions,
Whilst homely drabs in coaches ride,
    Brought up to town on pillions.

Few men, who follow reason's rules,
  Grow fat with South-Sea diet,
Young rattles and unthinking fools
  Are those that flourish by it,
Old musty jades and pushing blades,
  Who've least consideration,
Grow rich apace, whilst wiser heads
  Are struck with admiration.

A race of men, who t'other day
  Lay crush'd beneath disasters,
Are now by stock brought into play,
  And made our lords and masters.
But should our South-Sea Babel fall,
  What numbers would be frowning!
The losers then must ease their gall
  By hanging or by drowning.

Five hundred millions, notes and bonds,
  Our stocks are worth in value;
But neither lie in goods or lands
  Or money, let me tell ye.
Yet though our foreign trade is lost,
  Of mighty wealth we vapour,
When all the riches that we boast
  Consist in scraps of paper.

BUBBLE POEM.

There is a gulf where thousands fell,
  Here all the bold advent'rers came,
A narrow sound, tho' deep as hell,
  'Change Alley is the dreadful name.

Nine times a day it ebbs and flows,
  Yet he that on the surface lies,
Without a pilot seldom knows
  The time it falls, and when 'twill rise.

Subscribers here by thousands float,
  And justle one another down;
Each paddling in his leaky boat,
  And here they fish for gold, and drown.

Now buried in the depth below,
  Then mounted up to heav'n again,
They real and stagger to and fro,
  At their wits' end, like drunken men.

Meantime, secure on Garr'way's cliffs,
  A savage race by shipwrecks fed,
Lie waiting for the founder'd skiffs,
  And strip the bodies of the dead.

As fishes on each other prey,
  The great ones swallowing up the small,
So fares it in the Southern Sea;
  But whale directors eat up all.

While some build castles in the air,
  Directors build 'em in the seas;
Subscribers plainly see 'em there,
  For fools will see as wise men please.

Thus by directors we are told,
  Pray, gentlemen, believe your eyes,
Our ocean's cover'd o'er with gold—
  Look round about, how thick it lies.

Oh! would these patriots be so kind,
  Here in the deep to wash their hands;
Then, like Pactolus, we should find,
  The sea indeed had golden sands.

The nation too, too late will find,
  Computing all their cost and trouble,
Directors' promises but wind,
  South Sea, at best, a mighty bubble.

Swift.

THE JAIL BIRD.

Behold a poor, dejected wretch,
  Who kept a *S.-Sea coach* of late,
But now is glad to humbly catch
  A penny at the prison grate.

'Tis strange one set of knaves should sour
  A nation fam'd for wealth and wit,
But stranger still that men in power
  Should give a sanction to the cheat.

What ruin'd numbers daily mourn,
  Their groundless hopes, and follies past,
Yet see not how the tables turn,
  Or where their money flies at last.

Fools lost, when the directors won,
  But now the poor directors loose;
And where the S.-Sea stock will run,
  Old Nick, the first projector, knows.

THE DUTCH BUBBLERS.

The Dutch, who once were thought to be
  A crafty generation,
Are grown as foolish now we see,
  As any neighb'ring nation.
They copy England, England France,
  In vile destructive bubbles,
And ev'ry idle fraud advance,
  That can augment their troubles.
Three nations sure were never curs'd
  Before with such a madness,
That raises joyful hopes at first,
  But terminates in sadness.

'CHANGE ALLEY.

Thus with like haste thro' diff'rent paths they run,
Some to undo, and some to be undone.

See with what haste unthinking fools are running,
To humour knaves and gratify their cunning;
All seem transported with a joyful madness,
But soon their mighty hopes will turn to sadness.

CARDINAL WOLSEY IN THROGMORTON STREET, E.C.

Farewell, a long farewell to speculation!
This is the state of mines —
To-day they put forth prospectuses of hope,
To-morrow float, and bear their puffed-up premiums
    thick upon them.
The third day comes reaction: Then a fall;
And when they think, good easy public, surely
Their riches are a ripening—crash they go,
And then they "fail," as I do. I have ventured
Like many hard-up fools, that buy on credit,
This many fortnights on a sea of gold mines;
But far beyond my means. My note of hand
Has lost its moral weight, and now has left me
Ruined, but full of "tips," and to the mercy
Of a rigged market that has broke under me.
Vain, crushing "wires" and ore-assays I hate ye!
I feel my eyes wide opened. Oh! how wretched
Is that poor man who trusts Directors' ruses!
There is between the "tip" that we would act on—
That bait of gay promoters—and a profit,
More pangs and losses than the public wot of.
And when we "fail" we turn out busted men,
Never to rise again!   [*Exit weeping.*

Financial News, March 14th, 1887.

It is a strange anomaly that the more easy money becomes, the greater abundance there is of hard cash.

"Apollo Belvedere."—*1876.*

DIAMONDS *v.* PASTE.

A very popular member happens to be a good judge of precious stones. He used to be continually worried by members asking him to value, or give his opinion, of their purchases. At last he got tired of looking at rubbish, and when the next fellow asked him to value a diamond, he said, "What stone is it?"

"A diamond, of course, and of the purest water too; why do you ask?"

"Oh, I like to know what you think it is."

"How much is it worth?"

"Well, if it is *paste* I should say about 23*s.*, but if it is a *diamond* it's worth *nothing.*"

HOW IT IS DONE.

"What's this property of yours?" asked the innocent promoter.

"The Buckwheat Consolidated," replied the newly-arrived Yankee vendor.

"And where is it?"

"Here, on the map."

"Developed?"

"Well, rather; what are you giving me? It's got a ditch, a mill-site, a blacksmith's shop, and the finest boarding-house in the district."

"What is the price; the real inside price?"

"Half-a-million dollars—a hundred thousand pounds. And, say, you can just bet it will earn dividends on three hundred thousand pounds."

"What does the ore assay?"

"Well, I forget; it's either eight ounces to the ton, or eight tons to the ounce—I have forgotten which."

"What about directors?"

"Well, I can get a good American board—the pound-keeper in our town, a notary public at Podunk, and the coroner, who is an ex-alderman, at New Babylon. If you can get a Bank of England director and a couple of lords, I guess we can work it."

"I guess so," replied the promoter.

And the two adjourned to the Bodega basement to draft the prospectus.—*Financial News.*

A PANIC IN GOLD SHARES.

One per cent., five per cent.,
    Ten per cent., downward,
Into the Stock Exchange
    Rushed the six hundred.
No time to reason why,
No time to make reply,
"Sell! sell!" the only cry.
Into the Stock Exchange
    Rushed the six hundred.

Brokers to right of them,
Brokers to left of them,
Brokers in front of them
    Bellowed and thundered.
Bulls could not stem the tide,
Bears could not run or hide,
Few laughed, but many cried.
Into the Stock Exchange
    Rushed the six hundred.

Natal Mercury, September 14th, 1887.

PUNCH ON THE RAILWAY MANIA, 1845.

The year 1845 is known as the "year of the railway mania." People in every station of life seemed to have lost their senses and to have blindly rushed into every mad and rotten speculation brought under their notice by unscrupulous rogues. Many fortunes were made and many were lost. It was simply a repetition of the South-Sea Bubble. The history of those stirring times has been written by capable pens, and certainly deserves perusal. *Punch* for 1845, of course, contains many references to the mania. One full-page cartoon shows "Diogenes looking for an honest man in Capel Court." Another exhibits Punch and some friends "Stag-hunting in Capel Court." Again, we see a picture of Prince Albert looking very disconsolate, and the Queen asking him : " Pray tell me, Albert, have *you* any Railway Scrip?"

The following extracts are included in this work, as showing the spirit of the times :—

MONEY MARKET REPORT.

In the railway share market there is a tendency to go up, and it is probable that it will be all up with a great many in a week or two. In the foreign market, yesterday was settling day, and pawnbroker's scrip was in extensive demand to meet the claims made by the bulls and the bears on the geese and the donkeys. In order to satisfy the public appetite for speculation, a few new lines have been projected, the shares in which require a deposit of only five shillings; and we understand that at several of the larger schools the woman who goes round with the sweet-stuff is allowed to take a limited quantity of railway scrip in one corner of her basket, for the accommodation of juvenile jobbers.—April 12th, 1845.

Among the speculations at present in progress is a Great Libyan Desert and West of England Junction Arabian Sand Association, for the purpose of supplying England and the Continent of Europe with sand-paper.

A footman, lately in the service of a much-respected family of Berkeley Square, has just retired from service, having made £30,000 in six months by speculating in railway shares.

Thackeray wrote a long poem on this event.

"I say, Jim, vot's a Panic ?"
" Blow'd if I know; but there's von to be seen in the City."

November 1st, 1845.

SIGNS OF THE TIMES.

Two large stags have been put up at the Albert Gate. Since we are on the head of stags, we take this opportunity of contradicting a rumour that has been too much about, of a new order of merit being instituted in England, to be called "The Royal Order of the Stag."—September 27th, 1845.

THE STAGS.

A DRAMA OF TO-DAY.

Dramatis Personæ: TOM STAG, a Retired Thimblerigger; JIM STAG, an Unfortunate Costermonger.

(TOM *dictates to* JIM.)

Name in full . . . "Victor Wellesly Delancy."
Residence . . . . "Stagglands, Bucks."
Profession . . . . "Major-General, K.C.B., K.T.S., K.S.W."
Reference . . . . { "His Grace The Duke of Wellington.
{ "Sir Robert Peel. Coutts & Co."

"That'll do. Now, Mary, a vafer; and, Jim, I don't mind standing a pint of 'alf-and-'alf."—August 30th, 1845.

THE STAGS STAGGERED.

In consequence of the tremendous rush of stags into Capel Court, a rail is to be erected, to keep them off, by the authorities at the Stock Exchange. They will give the stags a rail of their own, on which they will be at full liberty to speculate.—October 4th, 1845.

A RAILWAY PANIC.

The *Boulogne News* emphatically calls upon the public to refrain from railway speculation, on the ground that many schemes will be unfinished for want of necessary iron. To say the truth, we do not anticipate a stoppage from want of *iron*, though we expect there will some day or other be a frightful smash for want of *tin*.—October 11th, 1845.

SONG OF THE STAG.

The Railway lists proclaim the fact,
"Deposits paid this morn;"
All who have cash must sign the act,
All who have none must mourn.
Bulls, bears, around the alley throng,
It is the settling day;
Then raise the burden of our song,
At last the Stag must pay!

HOUSE SCRAPS.

Lists, prices current, pass around,
    Their talk is of the Rail;
The alley echoes with the sound,
    And Capel Court looks pale.
The banks fill with an anxious throng,
    And money's stiff, they say;
The settling's come—too true our song,
    At last the Stag must pay!

Poor Stag! for cash thy brokers bore,
    And rueful is thy face;
All thy addresses serve no more,
    Thy rigs are out of place.
But when the alley runs thee down
    As a tremendous doo,
'Tis sad to think that half the town
    Is just as bad as you.
                  October 11th, 1845.

LOST OR STRAYED!

Whereas, the Railway Board of Trade has not been heard of for months; anyone who can give information as to its present locality will materially oblige a large circle of stags, who are most anxious to know whether the said Board is still in existence. If so, it is earnestly implored to communicate instantly with its disconsolate friends in Capel Court.—October 25th, 1845.

SONG OF THE RAILWAY MANIAC.

This is my left hand—this my right;
    These are my eyes, my nose, my mouth;
I can discern the day from night;
    There lies the north and there the south.
Shake not the head then—cry not "Hush!"
    Lay not the finger on the lip.
Away! Unhand me! Let me rush
    In quest of railway shares and scrip.

Ha! ha! 'Tis you are mad, I say:
    You talk to me of three per cents.,
Consols? Pooh, nonsense! What are they?
    You prate of mortgages and rents—
I tell you there are no such things—
    Nay, do not threaten chains and whip;
They've flown away with paper wings,
    And left us only shares and scrip.

What! mind my business? Fellow dear,
    You'll find yourself in Bedlam soon.
Hark! Let me whisper in your ear:
    Look! There's my business, in the moon!
That's where all occupation's fled;
    Gone, presto! with hop, jump, and skip.
How now, then, can I earn my bread,
    Except by railway shares and scrip?

Get in my debts? Ho, how you rave!
    Who thinks of paying what he owes?
No! tell me not that he's a knave:
    In scrip and shares the money goes.
Mark yonder man—he's a trustee,
    With others' stock in guardianship.
Where is it? Ha, my friend! you'll see
    All sunk in railway shares and scrip.

Stick to the shop? What shop? I've none!
    Defend me—how the madman stares!
I tell you there's no shop but one:
    The office where they sell you shares.
You have a tailor—want a coat—
    Go, order it : you'll find that Snip,
I'll bet you, sir, a ten-pound note,
    Will only measure you for scrip.

I am not mad! I am not mad!
    See where the shares on whirlwinds fly.
Off! Give me back the wings I had,
    To mount and catch them in the sky.
Maniac, I say, you torture me!
    You crush me in that iron grip!
Madman, away! and leave me free
    To chase my railway shares and scrip.
                      October 25th, 1845.

TO BE SOLD.

A Railway Call, which may be had on very reasonable terms. It is well adapted for anyone who is going on a very long voyage, and does not intend to come back again. Particulars may be had at the sign of the " Bald-faced Stag," or at the temporary office of the owner, on the third curbstone from Capel Court, opposite the Bank of England.—November 1st, 1845.

TO THE STAGGING WORLD.

Messrs. Nathan beg to inform their friends and the public that they have fitted up extensive premises opposite the Exchange, where costumes of every description likely to inspire confidence will be hired out to gents intending to sign for railway scrip in two or more characters, at a very low figure.

LIST OF PRICES.

	£	s.	d.
Bishop's Costume—Apron, Hat, Black Silks, and Buckles, complete	1	1	0
Low Church Rector—Black Tights, Short Gaiters, &c.; False Calves, if required	0	15	0
Puseyite Divine—Long Black Single-breasted Coat, narrow Collar	0	10	6
Sporting Banker of the Old School—Blue Coat, brass buttons, Yellow Waistcoat, Drab Pants, or Shorts	0	15	0
Watch Chain and Bunch of Seals, extra	0	5	0
Flash West-End Gent—Cutaway Coat, Velvet Vest, Railway Pants	0	15	0
Mosaic Jewellery for ditto...	0	5	0
Country Gents, Widows, K.C.B.'s, and Comfortable Tradesmen got up at five minutes' notice in the most accurate manner, each	0	10	6

October 25th.

VERSES ON A YOUNG LADY STAG.

Little Kitty Lorimer,
   Fair, and young, and witty,
What has brought your ladyship
   Rambling to the City?

All the Stags in Capel Court
   Saw her lightly trip it;
All the lads of Stock Exchange
   Twigg'd her muff and tippet.

With a sweet perplexity,
   And a mystery pretty,
Threading through Threadneedle Street,
   Trots the little Kitty.

What was my astonishment—
   What was my compunction—
When she reached the offices
   Of the Didland Junction?

Up the Didland stairs she went,
   To the Didland door, sir;
Porters, lost in wonderment,
   Let her pass before, sir.

"Madam," says the old chief clerk,
   "Sure, we can't admit ye."
"Where's the Didland Junction deed?"
   Dauntlessly says Kitty.

"If you doubt my honesty,
  Look at my receipt, sir."
Up then jumps the old chief clerk,
  Smiling as he meets her.

Kitty at the table sits
  (Whither the old clerk leads her);
"*I deliver this*," she says,
  "*As my act and deed, sir.*"

When I heard these funny words
  Come from lips so pretty;
This, I thought, should surely be
  Subject for a ditty.

What! are ladies stagging it?
  Sure, the more's the pity;
But I've lost my heart to her—
  Naughty little Kitty!
                November 1st, 1845.

THE RAILWAY COMMITTEE MART.

Railway Committees in want of Directors are requested to apply at the British and Foreign Destitute. There is always a good supply kept on hand, and no questions asked. The charge is one hundred shares for an Esquire, and fifty more for a real Knight. Secretaries in any quantity, and prospectuses got up at an hour's notice. N.B.—A dictionary on the premises.—November 1st.

JAQUES IN CAPEL COURT.

        All the world are stags!
Yea, all the men and women merely jobbers!
They have their brokers and their share accounts;
And one man in his time tries many lines,
The end being total ruin. First, the greenhorn,
Dabbling and dealing in a lucky spec;
And then the prosperous seller, with his profits
And joyous winning face, buying like mad,
Unwilling to sell out; and then, the loser,
Sighing like a furnace, with a woful prospect
Of the next settling day. Then the director,
Full of strange schemes, and lodged at the West-End,
Keeping a cab, and sudden growing rich,—
Getting a bubble reputation
Even in Capel Court. And then the bankrupt,
With his debts' schedule large, and no assets:

By all his decent friends entirely cut,—
Full of bad scrip, and fertile of fresh schemes,
And so he plays his game. The sixth step sinks
Into the low and herring-gutted stag,
With spectacles on nose and list in hand:
His youthful gains all spent, the world too wide-
Awake to be ta'en in, and his long line
Of hapless creditors that idly wait
And whistle for their cash. Last scene of all,
That ends this sad but common history,
Is—Union pauperism, and oakum-picking;
Sans beer, sans beef, sans tea, sans everything.

November 1st, 1845.

We understand the Thames Tunnel Company is ready to dispose of its shaft. We should like to know what has become of all the shafts of ridicule that were at one time being constantly hurled at it. If these were collected together and sold by auction, a very capital dividend might yet be returned to the shareholders.—November 15th, 1845.

THE SHARE MARKET.

The Grand Northern and Eastern Clothes Line did not move a peg all the morning, and Great Trunks, which opened well, closed heavily. A juvenile stag, whose scrip was at half-discount, cried out piteously for his par, but got no attention.

* * * * * * * * *

A stag, dining near Capel Court, made a strange mistake the other day, which only proves that whatever is uppermost in the mind is sure to come out. He wanted some potatoes, but unwittingly cried out, "Here, Mary, bring me a plate of mashed railways."—November 15th, 1845.

THE IRON MARKET.

The demand for iron for the railroads is being sensibly felt in the feverish state of saucepans, which have risen to an alarming height within the last few weeks. A good tea-kettle, which was quoted in the New Cut as low as ninepence a month ago, has rushed up to a shilling, without the *coupon*, that is to say, with no lid to it. The buoyancy in gridirons has been quite frightful, for their resemblance to railway lines has made them the object of competition among various companies. Pokers were dreadfully firm, without the smallest probability of their yielding; and there being no chance of their giving way, there was a good deal of activity. With the exception, however, of pokers, there was very little stirring, for irons were flat, and people seemed afraid of burning their fingers.

November 22nd, 1845.

CAPEL COURT.

(Suggested by Alfred Tennyson's "Locksley Hall.")

Comrades, go and get your dinners, there's an eating-house at hand;
Leave me here, and when you want me, you will find me in the Strand.
'Tis the place, and all around it seems with recollection fraught;
Dreary kites are flying round me as I stand in Capel Court.
Capel Court, that in its precincts overlooks the herd of stags,
And the crowd of speculators, dressed in little more than rags.
Many a day I read the paper, ere I had retired to rest,
And it spoke of lots of railways, north to south and east to west.
Many a night I saw the prices, with the profits that were made—
Five, and six, and seven premium, upon shares with two pounds paid.
Here about the court I wandered, nourishing a hope sublime—
I might get a large allotment if I only wrote in time.
The prospectuses before me many a splendid scheme proposed,
And at once I wrote before the list of applications closed.
When I dipt into my pocket, my resources just to see,
All was blank, my purse was empty—empty as a purse could be!
And I said, " My worthy broker, speak, and speak the truth, I pray,
On my letters of allotment will you the deposit pay?"
On his cheek there came a colour, every feature growing bright,
And I thought " He's flush of money, everything will now be right."
Then he turn'd, his cheek-bone shaking, as he points, with winks and becks,
To the balance in his favour on the margin of the checks;
Saying, " I have lots of credit, with my banker I am strong!"
Saying, " Bring me your allotments; I will pay them, right or wrong."
Hope took up the pen in time, and wielding it with eager hands,
Fifty shares in every railway resolutely he demands.
Hope took up the stagging line, and at it went with all his might;
Writing, writing for allotments, morning, evening, noon, and night.
Many a morning, at his lodging, did he hear the top-bell ring,
Hoping it might be the postman, who some shares had come to bring.
Many a morning, in the City, did we go and get the scrips,
And the profits shared together when we sold the precious slips.
Oh, my broker, chicken-hearted! Oh, my broker, mine no more!
Oh! the horrid, horrid panic! What a—what a dreadful bore!

* * * * *

Oh! I see the crescent promise of my profit hath not set,
Ancient lines are at a premium, I may make a fortune yet.
However these things be, a long farewell to Capel Court;
I must cut before the settling, since for the account I've bought,
Comes a bubble from the distance, blackening with the City's smoke:
When it bursts, to those beneath it, 'twill not be at all a joke.
Let it fall on Capel Court, in cold water let it drizzle;
I've a long account to settle—which I can't—and so I mizzle.

November 22nd, 1845.

The fearful lull in the Share market has given rise to the following lullaby, which is now being sung by the stags of Capel Court, as they pace the deserted purlieus of the Stock Exchange :—

> Hush-a-by, broker, at Capel Court top,
> When the wind's raised the premiums will stop,
> When there's a breeze the premiums will fall,
> Down come the holders, the brokers, and all.

November 22nd, 1845.

NEW PROVERB.—Promises, like railway companies, are only made to be broken.

THE RAILWAY MANIA.

The first symptoms of the Railway Mania are idleness and inattention to business, and a neglect of study; the patient leaving good books to read the newspaper supplements. As the disorder progresses, the conversation becomes wild and incoherent, and remarkably disagreeable to all sane hearers, by running continually on Shares, Scrip, Premiums, and Grand Junctions, so as to resemble nothing but the confused jargon of Capel Court. By degrees, reason is prostrated, and the moral feelings are prevented, so that the sufferer becomes deprived of the power of taking care of himself, and the perception of what he owes to others. Under these circumstances he writes frantically for shares in lines that are, and always will be, imaginary, and, to purchase them, throws away all the money he has, and renders himself liable for much more. He sells out Three per Cents, mortgages houses and estates, disposes of his business, and commits various other acts of extravagance.

At length, his violence having become mischievous, he is confined; but, unfortunately, as his disorder is an unrecognised madness, his only asylum is the workhouse or the gaol.—November 22nd, 1845.

WANTON FELONY.

The *Times* of Saturday last contains an advertisement headed as follows:—"RAILWAY SCRIP STOLEN." Can a more gratuitous piece of dishonesty be imagined than such a theft, when waste paper is only twopence a pound?—November 27th, 1845.

RAILWAY INTELLIGENCE.

We understand that the largest transactions in scrip are at present confined to the marine-store dealers, who have lately taken up this branch of commerce with some alacrity. The placards in their windows now announce, that the best price is given for Capel Court stuff, as well as kitchen stuff. Instead of calling upon people to look up their old rags and waste paper, they are requested to look up their old letters of allotment and useless scrip, for which a liberal amount will be given.

December 6th, 1845.

THE RUNAWAY DIRECTORS.

The retreat of the directors is still going on, and we can only compare it to the celebrated running away of the Rifles after the breaking up of the lines. Are the poor stags to be left to go to the dogs? The only cuttings with which the railroad committee-men now appear to trouble themselves, is a general cutting away! The shareholders are singing—

> Oh, dear, what can the matter be?
> This is a shocking affair!
> They promised to bring out the Scrip at a premium,
> Which now is worth nothing per share.

December 6th, 1845.

THE STAG'S FAREWELL TO ENGLAND.

> My boat is on the strand,
>   My steamer's on the sea;
> I quit my native land—
>   America, for thee.
> My wig of red is on,
>   I've dyed my grizzled brow,
> My whiskers dark are gone,—
>   They will not know me now.
>
> My tender wife, adieu!—
>   Farewell, my little ones;
> And oh! farewell to you,
>   My poor deluded duns;
> And thou, too, even thou,
>   My tailor, sufferer poor,
> Wilt fruitless vengeance vow
>   'Gainst him thou'lt see no more.

December 6th, 1845.

RAILWAY GARDENING.

Do not scatter your money broadcast, but sow in good regular lines, unless for immediate use, when you may plant anywhere; but you must take care to be prepared for clearing out and getting in the crop as quickly as possible.—*Almanack*, 1846.

The extent of railway surveying has caused a certain popular query to be superseded. Instead of, " Has your mother sold her mangle?" the boys in the streets now ask, " Has your father sold his theodolite?"

January 3rd, 1846.

RIDDLE FOR THE CITY.

Oh! why, my friend, is a Joint-Stock
Concern like, yet unlike, a clock?
Because it may be wound up; when,
Alas! it doesn't go again.
December 19th, 1857.

THE LAY OF THE ALLOTTEE.

When I remember all the lines
    In which I've taken shares,
My mind the hopeless task resigns
    Of counting all my cares.
Woolmer and Toby is the cry,
    What can its meaning be?
An exile from my land I fly,
    Poor hapless Allottee!

Onwards, across the briny deep,
    Rolls the majestic ship;
I pace the deck, then sit and weep
    O'er piles of worthless scrip.
'Tis ever thus—'mid Time's advance,
    Crush'd hopes we're doom'd to see;
Bear me, ye billows, swift to France,
    Poor hapless Allottee!

They ask me the expense to share,
    Of outlay all their own;
How will the Secretary stare
    To find the victim flown!
From ribaldry on such a theme,
    Angry and hurt I flee;
Good Captain, pray put on the steam
    For the poor Allottee!

I stand at length upon the shore
    Of fair and courtly France;
I hear the breakers loudly roar,
    I see the billows dance.
Upon the pier I take a turn,
    Lonely I cannot be;
Each one I meet has been, I learn,
    A fellow Allottee!
May 9th, 1846

A. "I say, old fellow, lend me a sovereign for a few days."
B. "Very sorry, my dear boy! I only lend *one* sovereign and *that's out.*"

An old gentleman travelling on the South-Eastern Railway recently handed the ticket inspector half a ticket, and when asked for a whole one, said, "Its all right. I was under age when I started by this train."

SCENE—*Outside the House.*
Broker (to friendly jobber). "Bad times, old man! any luck?"
"No, confound it! I've stood here for four hours, and not been solicited once!"

BROKERS' RENTS.

Brokers' rents ceased to be collected by the Corporation of the City of London on the 29th September, 1886. These rents of £5 from each broker yielded an annual income to the Corporation of about £8,000. From the earliest times the Corporation exercised control over persons who acted as brokers. A statute of Edward I. enacted that there should be no brokers but those received and sworn by the Lord Mayor and Aldermen, and that "no stranger" should be permitted to take up the office of broker; consequently every broker had to become a freeman of the City. James I. granted to the citizens the privilege of "garbling spices" in the City, which brought a considerable profit. By an Act of Parliament, 6 Anne, cap. 16, this was abolished, and, in consideration of the loss of the profit, the City was allowed to impose a rent of 40*s.* per annum on every broker, which in the reign of George III. was increased to £5. After some time the brokers complained of the tax, and in 1870 they were relieved of the greater part of the supervision of the Court of Aldermen, but the rent remained. In 1884 the brokers intimated that they intended to introduce a Bill for the total abolition of the rents, and the Corporation agreed that if the rents were paid until this year they would not oppose the Bill. This was agreed to, and the Bill was passed unopposed.

HOUSE SCRAPS.

Our only Captain was ordering his company to fall back, in order to dress with the line, and gave the word "*Advance* three paces *backwards!* March!"

BUBBLE AND SQUEAK.

At the time that the bubble schemes were flourishing, in 1825, Mr. Abernethy met some friends who had risked large sums of money in one of those fraudulent speculations. They informed him that they were going to partake of a most sumptuous dinner, the expenses of which would be defrayed by the Company. "If I am not very much deceived," replied he, "you will have nothing but *bubble and squeak* in a short time."

A jobber, being asked to lend a friend a "quid," took out his book as though to enter a bargain; then, suddenly looking him very hard in the face, said, "Very sorry, but I find it's no good to me Haven't you tried elsewhere."

Sing hey! for the Bulls and Bears,
And ho! for the Turkey Cocks,
Sing Bonds, and Scrip and Shares,
Sing British and Foreign Stocks.

CLEARED OUT.

First Speculator. "Lima Tramway Bonds, what did you clear by them?"
Second Speculator. "My pockets."

HARD TIMES.

"Have you sufficient confidence in me to lend me a sovereign?"
"Oh! yes, I've the confidence, but I haven't the thick-un."

PROGRAMME
OF A
GRAND MINSTREL ENTERTAINMENT,
GIVEN IN AID OF THE
STOCK EXCHANGE CLERKS' PROVIDENT FUND,
AT
PRINCES' HALL, PICCADILLY, 23rd MAY, 1884.

PART I.
Overture	. . . .	By the COMPANY.
Ballad	. . "Fare thee well, Kitty dear" .	. J. M. BAZIN.
Comic Song .	. "Good-bye, Susan Jane" .	J. S. OAKENFULL.
Ballad	. . "Wait till the Clouds roll by" .	. W. ALLEN.
Ballad	. . "'Tis a Voice in the Air" .	. W. PHILLIPS.
Comic Song .	. "Oh! I'd like to be a Bird" .	. . T. TODD.
Ballad	. . "Come where my Love lies Dreaming" .	. G. EGAN.
Comic Song .	. "The Laughing Nigger" .	HAMILTON SCOTT.
Ballad	. . "'Tis only a Pansy Blossom" .	. T. DETMAR.
Ballad	. . "Call me back again" .	PELHAM H. ROOFF.
Comic Song .	. "Good-bye, Emily Jane" .	. WALTER PALLANT.
Descriptive Finale	. "The Sleigh Ride" . . .	. The COMPANY.

The Start—The Song on the Road—The Race Home.

Piano—SYDNEY DAVIS. *Stage Manager*—ARTHUR RAYMOND.

PART II.
Cornet Solo	. . . . A. ELLERTON.
Comic Duet	. . . . WALTER PALLANT & HAMILTON SCOTT.
Ballad	. . . . G. EGAN.
Pas de Big Boots	. . . . F. W. PRIOR.
Banjo Solo	. . . . HAMILTON SCOTT.
Black Board Sketches	. . . . F. C. GOULD.

During which the Band will play Mr. Vandervell's Gavotte—"IMMER-WIEDER."

To conclude with a short Sketch, entitled
"WANTED—AN ACTOR."

Mr. GRACE .	. . . (A Manager) .	. W. L. DE BOOS.
SNOW	. . . . (His Ill-used Servant) .	. HAMILTON SCOTT.
SAM BLOBBER	. . . (Anything you like) .	. WALTER PALLANT.

Vocalists.

Messrs. G. Davison.	W. Phillips.
J. F. Southwell.	Stanley Scott.
H. Bates.	G. Egan.
T. Detmar.	W. Allen.
H. Smith.	J. M. Bazin.
Pelham Rooff.	H. M. Marshall.

Instrumentalists.

Messrs. A. Lovey.	J. de la Mare.
H. G. Brown.	A. Ellerton.
J. Coldwells.	F. M. Wood.
H. Guy.	J. Clark.
G. D. Atkin.	A. Whitefield.
C. S. Smith.	Geo. Gray.
S. J. Smith.	W. Vandervell.
R. M. Phillipps.	T. Goldsborough.
J. Guy.	&c.

Corner Men: Bones—Messrs. HAMILTON SCOTT & J. S. OAKENFULL.
Tambourines—T. TODD & WALTER PALLANT.
Interlocutor—Mr. W. L. DE BOOS.

Manager—Mr. WALTER PALLANT. *Musical Director*—Mr. E. BROOKES.

The above entertainment was a tremendous success, nearly £150 was handed to the Clerks' Provident Fund. The 5s. stalls rose to 25s. premium before the date of performance. It was acknowledged the jolliest evening since the vocal competition, Oxley v. Owen, in 1862.

A CAPACITY.

A lucky speculator, paying his daughter a visit at school, enquired what progress she had made in her education. The governess answered, "Pretty fair, she is very attentive; if she wants anything it is a *capacity*, but for *that* deficiency you know we must not blame *her*."

"No, madam," replied the speculator, "but I blame *you* for not having mentioned it before. I can well afford my daughter a *capacity*, and I beg you to order one immediately."

INQUEST EXTRAORDINARY.

Died suddenly—surprised at such a rarity!
Verdict—Saw Moses do a little bit of charity.

Many years ago, a party of ten *bon-vivants* met to celebrate a lucky *coup* made by one of them. After the feast the bill was presented, but the amount appeared so enormous to one of the company (not quite so far gone as the rest) that he protested it was impossible so many bottles could have been drunk by seven persons. "Very true, sir," said the waiter, "but your honour forgets the three gentlemen *under the table*."

A broker (noted for his bumptiousness), on his way through the House, said to some jobbers:—

"Haw! When I come in here, you fellows swarm round me like flies round a honey-pot."

"Yes, Mr. Blank! but don't forget that flies also swarm round *something else*."

VALUE OF STOCK EXCHANGE SECURITIES.

The total value of securities quoted in the official list on December 31st, 1886, amounted to:—

Authorised issue.	Present amount.
£6,332,247,172.	£5,676,374,158.

The above amount does not, by any means, represent the value of the stocks and shares *dealt in* on the Stock Exchange. Scores of mines, dozens of foreign railways, and many other companies not being quoted.

If we take the "present amount" and divide equally amongst every man, woman, and child on the face of the earth, each one would receive a trifle over £4. What a chance for the Socialists!

RINGING THE CHANGES.

At a tavern, one night,
Messrs. *Moore, Strange,* and *Wright,*
Met to drink, and good thoughts to exchange:
Says *Moore,* "Of us three,
The whole town will agree,
There is only one knave, and that's *Strange.*"
"Yes," says *Strange* (rather sore),
"I'm sure there's one *Moore,*
A most terrible knave and a bite,
Who cheated his mother,
His sister, and brother."—
"O, yes," replied *Moore,* "that is *Wright.*"

THE HANDSOMEST MAN IN THE HOUSE.

Society offered a dozen of champagne to the handsomest man in the House. The competition was opened in October, 1886, and closed November 13th. Anybody was allowed to send as many coupons as he liked—of course the coupons could only be had by buying the paper. The following results were published in the issue for November 20th, 1886 :—

H. Maas	1,364	F. Milbank	409	Ed. Fenner	2
E. Herman	1,357	Ted Stearns	378	Wm. Willes	2
Chas. H. Snell	1,342	B. C. Stock	240	W. F. Hensley	2
H. K. Paxton	1,079	Ernest Walford	233	James Skinner, Jr.	1
Sir M. D. Gordon	1,056	F. W. Petch	223	Alf. Emberson	1
Wm. J. Gordon	1,027	W. C. Meates	189	Bertie Barker	1
Eustratius Ralli	989	C. J. Mocatta	172	H. E. Fitzclarence	1
Tom Nickalls	959	Spenser Nettleton	123	Edward Godefroi	1
W. H. Mitchell	947	J. Wilson	119	H. Panmure Gordon	1
H. K. Ricardo	937	David Soloman	115	Louis Hyams	1
E. C. Waller	930	Percy Elias Davis	112	D. R. Hammond	1
John Pyemont	918	Joseph R. Starling	109	H. W. Jefferson	1
T. Norris Oakley	879	J. Renton, Jr.	96	Julian Joseph	1
Walter Weil	856	Geo. Lacy Hillier	57	A. Kindell	1
Geo. Meane	809	L. J. Baker	34	W. B. Carne	1
Ellis Willes	805	Albert Shackel	6	Hosier Morgan	1
Chas. Hoblyn	737	Tom Cuvelje	5	Arthur J. Phillips	1
Lionel Bulteel	654	J. Kerwin	5	Lewis Powell	1
W. B. Puckle	653	J. Oakley Maunde	3	J. S. Thompson	1
Jack Short	636	D. Richardson	3	A. L. Wildy	1
F. Knollys	605	W. Thompson	3	James Gingold	1
R. M. Nicholas	537	Montague Barron	2	G. O. Layton	1
Godefroi Ingall	501	H. R. Bullock	2	Michael Marks	1
Ed. Baker	467	Lodovick Cottrell	2	J. Thomson King	1

And 19 others, one vote each.

A SHARP TRICK.

A needy speculator wrote to several brokers, asking them to sell a certain stock. Not liking the references, and hoping to catch a "sharper," the brokers each agreed to send him a *stamped transfer*, with a request for his signature, and the certificates of the stock. The "needy one" *swore off the stamps and pocketed the "swag."*

A wit being asked on the failure of his bank, "Where you not upset?"—replied, "No! I only lost my balance."

A COOLER.

A member having dined well, but not wisely, entered a restaurant and attempted to open a "hand-grenade fire-extinguisher."

Barmaid (excitedly). "For goodness sake, don't touch that; it is a fire-extinguisher!"

Member. "Oh! I thought it was lemonade. Are you certain it will extinguish fire?"

Barmaid. "Yes, sir!"

Member. "Then I'll take half-a-dozen. Handy to put in my *coffin*, you know."

OLD MEMBERS.

In spite of the worry and excitement, some members live to be old men. One of the oldest, still in the House, was in the French army when Napoleon I. was retreating from Moscow.

Sir Robert Carden, Bart., M.P., has been in the House for 70 years and is still hale and hearty.

John Riva, after leading an active life in Change Alley, retired to Venice, where he is reported to have died at the patriarchal age of 118.

He was a mild youth, just fresh from school, and when some naughty members told him a little story, he did not even smile, but simply said that he did not understand the story, he supposed it had a "*Dublin Tender*" to it.

FAMILIARITY.

The following illustrates the familiar manner in which some masters and clerks treat each other:—A member once asked his clerk to take a parcel to London Bridge Station and wait for him there. The clerk, not seeing his governor about the station, asked a porter if he had seen a "long, scraggy, carrotty-looking devil hanging about anywhere?" but before the porter could answer, a well-known voice was heard on the other side of a tremendous pile of luggage, "All right, Charlie my boy, here I am."

A member, noted for his heavy drinking habits, was asked by a friend to do him a favour, and, on his asking what it was he could do for him, his friend said: "Oh, just lend me about two ounces of your *breath*, I want to *kill my neighbour's cat*."

Pourquoi Williams spends a week at Boulogne.—*20th December, 1870.*

A BIG RISE.

A well-known speculator was sitting in a friend's office, one hot day last summer, and during the conversation he informed his friend that he had picked up a cheap thing during the winter. "It stood at 33 then, and yesterday it touched 84."

"By Jove! what a lucky fellow you are. What was it?"

"Only a thermometer," was the quiet reply.

THE MAN-I-JIRS OF THE GREAT
Discovered in

TEMPLE OF THE BULL AND BEAR.
Sit-tee Desert.

A worthy member one day walked into the American market with an order to *sell* 100 Eries. He asked the price in 100 shares of a well-known jobber, who replied "⅞-⅝ sir, and I'll bet you half-a-crown that I know what you want to do."

"All right."

"Well, you want to *sell* a hundred."

"No I don't," says the broker, thinking he was certain of his 2s. 6d.

"All right then, here's your half-a-crown, and I shall *sell you* 100 Eries at ⅞; if you're not a *seller* you must be a *buyer*."

Seeing he was caught in his own trap he retired, amidst the laughter of the market.

The following lines were "stuck up" in the House about the time when Albert Grant was made a Baron:—

> "Monarchs grant titles, but honour they can't,
> Rank, without honour, makes a { barren / Baron } Grant.

HOW TO COLLECT A DIVIDEND.

In the early days of rail-roading in Missouri, a six-foot stranger, with a bad look in his eye, one day entered a station, pulled out ten shares, and inquired of the stationmaster if there were any dividends on the stock?

"Never heard of any," was the reply.

"Didn't anybody ever try to collect dividends?"

"If they did try they didn't get anything."

"I guess this 'ere stock ought to pay 10 per cent., here's $1,000, 10 per cent. will be $100. I've held these sheers three months, so that'll be $25. Pardner, I want my divy."

"But I've nothing to do with it; you must go to St. Louis."

"Too fur away! I'm going to collect right here and save time, so count it out."

The stranger here toyed with a six-shooter, with an expression which meant business. The agent didn't take three minutes in counting out the money, which the stranger took, and walked out, with the remark, that he never invested in any stock paying less than 10 per cent.; and didn't believe in cumulative dividends. This was the only dividend paid by the company for thirteen years.

> For since the Duke of Argyle
> Has consider'd it worth while
>   To bring his son up to the scratch,
>   I believe we may boast
>   We have found him a post
>   Which in Scotland nothing can match.

A JOKE.

Some years ago, when some distinguished Belgians were on a visit to London and Wimbledon, three jobbers played a capital joke. The Belgians were desirous of visiting the House, but the committee or managers would not give them permission to do so. Some members, headed by Mr. M——, interested themselves in the matter, and got the permit for their admission. The three jokers, Harry Brown, Bill Eykyn, and another, went up to May's and got rigged out in the most awful costumes they could find, and then came down to the House in a "four-wheeler." Of course, the waiters admitted them, and they created much excitement. Mr. M—— was engaged in showing them round when a party of the real Belgians arrived, and the jokers were obliged to beat a hasty retreat.

FIVE PER CENT. FOR CASH.

A broker, who died a very wealthy man, was always looked upon with suspicion by the other members of the House on account of his very miserly habits, he barely allowing himself enough food to keep body and soul together. A few days before he died he sent for the overseers of his parish and informed them that he had left in his will £1,000 for the relief of the poor, and eagerly inquired whether they would not allow him some discount for prompt payment. Upon their agreeing to give 5 per cent. discount for cash, he at once drew a cheque on his banker for £950, to everybody's satisfaction.

THE SHARE MARKET.

The Hungerford and Belvedere Suspension shares are flat, but the holders are flatter. The report that a new pile had been driven in caused some excitement, which was soon allayed by an authenticated statement of the fact, that old Thames was so extremely obstinate, that he had scarcely been got out of the bed of the coffer before he tumbled in again.

The Chelsea Chain-pier scrip has rallied, and a shareholder who had thrown his shares into the dust-hole has had them looked for among the rubbish, with a view to giving them another trial. The Chelsea Emigration Society, for colonising Battersea Fields and draining all the flats in the neighbourhood of Wandsworth, has been broken up. Their chief object was to restore the ancient order of Jolly Young Watermen, but they have failed signally in this bold experiment.—*Punch*, 1843.

* * * * *

Bullion was scarce in the early part of the day, but a party came in towards the close of business with change for a five pound note, which gave a fresh impetus to all the transactions.

* * * * *

Cash is said to be easy, which accounts for there being no hard cash to be got in any quarter.— 1843.

A DUET.

A certain member, who had made a considerable fortune in the House through some lucky specs, although it was hinted that he had some difficulty in writing his own name, determined to have his daughter educated regardless of expense, so sent her to a well-known finishing establishment, where young ladies are taught "a great deal about nothing and nothing about everything." When she came home for the holidays, her beloved father asked a few friends round to spend the evening, with the view of showing off her wonderful accomplishments. After dinner she played one or two "show pieces," greatly to her parent's delight. "Maria, dear, play the piece you were playing last night," said her fond pa.

"But I can't, pa! That was a *duet*."

"That doesn't matter, play it!"

A DISAPPOINTMENT.

"What means this crowd, so dense and denser yet,
That Baring's solemn portal has beset?
    What do they hold so dear?
Has some great western nation once more sought
For English loans, perchance too dearly bought?"
    They answered me: "'Tis beer!
Not the light sparkling foam of Bass's ale,
Not even Allsopp—his 'East India pale;'
    'Tis honest Guinness stout,
Which for three weary livelong nights and days,
With eager greed and venturesome amaze
    Has turned the world about.
Be it the firm debenture, (money lent),
Be it the winsome preference (6 per cent.!)
    Be it the hopeful share—
Be it whate'er it may, our simple task
Is the allotment due to us to ask—
    If aught there be to spare."

"Give me a form! a cheque!" I cried; "th' amount
My bankers hold I scarcely need to count.
    I sell whate'er I get!"
My cheque was cashed. All seemed to promise well.
I sold; and then came all I had to sell,—
    A letter of regret!

        St. James's Gazette, November 10th, 1886.

I have been taken for a merchant upon the Exchange for above these ten years, and sometimes pass for a Jew in the assembly of stock brokers in Jonathan's.—*The Spectator*, No. 1., March 1st, 1710.

CANZONET FOR THE CITY.

The ocean now runs mountains high,
   Now sinks, a level plain;
The money market is, though dry,
   Just like the watery main.
It fluctuates to the same extent,
   In proof whereof we see
That interest has, from ten per cent,
   Now tumbled down to three.
                  Punch, February 20th, 1858.

THE BURDEN OF THE CITY.

"The public shows but little inclination to invest."—*Weekly Paper.*

We don't know what the matter is; we've lots of pleasant lines—
   The Suakim and the Berber route, and many a dozen more;
We've Peruvians and Egyptians, and gold and silver mines,
   That investors might make trial of—they've often tried before;
And there's Tramways, and Coal Companies, and Anglo-Argentines,
   There are Japanese and Mexicans, quite equal to the best;
And yet for all these stocks of ours there's nobody that pines,
   And the public shows but little inclination to invest!

There's our festive Indian Railways, such as Quetta and Penjdeh,
   Why the public will not look at them one really can't conceive,
For the Russians—on a largish map—are leagues on leagues away,
   And perhaps they're only joking and a-laughing in their sleeve.
Then we've Chilians, Brazilians, and Stocks of Uruguay,
   And a China Loan, the newest out, and very cheap confessed;
And we've gas at Monte Video, and canals at Santa Fé,
   Yet the public shows but little inclination to invest.

What on earth men put their savings in, for savings there must be,
   Is a problem, but their "caution" seems a frivolous pretence,
When we've telephones and telegraphs by land, and air, and sea,
   And a highly eligible stock, like Ottoman Defence.
But they won't defer to our "Deferreds" or choose our "Preference,"
   For "An. Am. Brush Electric Lights" they have but little zest;
Though folk "circular" and advertise, regardless of expense,
   Yet the public shows but little inclination to invest.
                  Punch, March 28th, 1885.

Epitaph for a Stock-Broker—"Waiting for a Rise.

A BRILLIANT IDEA.

A French millionaire, at the point of death, sent for his nephew who was on the Bourse, and said, " Pierre, people have accused me of being a miser, and have asked what use would all my money be to me when I die, as I couldn't take it away with me. Now, Pierre, I will leave you all my money if you promise to put 100,000 frs. in my coffin and bury them with me." Pierre promised, and shortly afterwards the old miser died. Pierre at once began to think how he could save the 100,000 frs., and yet carry out his uncle's instructions. At last a brilliant idea struck him. He drew a *cheque to order* for 100,000 frs. and placed it in the coffin, so tha the old man " could *cash it when he wanted it.*"

3 per cent. Reduced.

BAD LUCK.

" Hallo Brown! how are you? I haven't seen you for an age; how's business?"

" Beastly bad, luck's dead against me, here, I've been investing and investing, and done nothing but lose."

" Indeed, I'm very sorry to hear you say so."

" I believe that if I've lost a shilling I've lost over £80,000."

" Really?"

" Yes; and that's not the worst, for nearly two hundred pounds of it was my own money."

THE BROKER'S CLERK.

When first I came to London town,
    A simple country joker,
I went to work with Mr. Brown,
    A most respected broker.
He dealt in Stocks, Reduced, Consols,
    And corporation pledges;
The work was quite a change for oi
    From trimming-up of hedges.
Oh, Lord! how well he treated us,
    He gave us lots of victuals;
And there was joy in his employ,
    All life was beer and skittles.
Ah! they were merry happy times,
    While markets kept on rising,
And everything went upwards till
    The prices were surprising.
Then every settling day at one,
    Two good half-crowns he gave us,
And all expense and trouble he
    Would do his best to save us.
Then Smith, my fellow clerk, explained
    "The Bulls are coining money,"
"And Brown's a Bull," I thought it strange
    That he should talk so funny.
Then Brown looked down, and went about
    With features marked with care;
And Smith irreverently declared
    "The fool should be a Bear."
But one fine morning Brown collapsed;
    They took him off to jail;
And I returned to rustic life
    To wield my father's flail.
No more the gay and festive crown
    Was shelled out for the dinner,
We didn't get another Brown,
    As I'm a living sinner.

OPINION OF STOCK-JOBBERS, ABOUT 1715.

"Its a complete system of knavery, founded in fraud, born of deceit and nourished by trick, cheat, wheedle, forgeries, falsehoods, and all sorts of delusions; coining false news, whispering imaginary terrors, and preying upon those they have elevated or depressed."

The lowest price consols ever touched was in 1798, viz., $47\frac{1}{4}$; and the highest, $103\frac{3}{4}$ on 31st May, 1887.

"Statesmen and patriots ply alike the stocks,
Peeress and butler share alike the box;
And judges job, and bishops bite the town;
And mighty dukes pack cards for half-a-crown."—*Pope.*

ORIGIN OF THE BLACK-BOARD.

"The origin of the black-board—that moral pillory—of the Stock Exchange, occurred in 1787. 'There were no less than 25 lame ducks,' said the *Whitehall Evening News*, 'who waddled out of the Alley.' Their deficiency was estimated at £250,000; and it was upon this occasion the above plan was first proposed, and a very full meeting of the members resolved that those who did not either pay their deficiencies or name their principals, should be publicly exposed on a black-board to be ordered for the occasion. Thus the above deficiencies—larger than had been previously known—alarmed the gentlemen of Change Alley, and produced that system which is yet regarded with wholesome awe."—*Francis, on the Stock Exchange.*

Inscription on a copper-plate placed beneath the first stone of the first building erected exclusively for the business of the Stock Exchange, May 18th, 1801 :—

"On the 18th of May, in the year 1801, and forty-one of George III., the first stone of this building—erected, by private subscription, for the transaction of business in the public funds—was laid, in the presence of the proprietors and under the direction of William Hammond, William Steer, Thomas Roberts, Griffith Jones, William Grey, Isaac Hensley, Jo. Brackshaw, John Capel, and John Barnes, managers; James Peacock, architect. At this æra, the first of the union between Great Britain and Ireland, the public funded debt had accumulated in five successive reigns to £552,730,924. The inviolate faith of the British nation, and the principles of the constitution, sanction and secure the property embarked in this undertaking. May the blessing of that constitution be secured to the latest posterity!"

TWO GOOD INVESTMENTS.

During the company mania in 1825-6, when the "stags" were ready for every new venture, a company was started for making gold. The shares were all greedily taken, and it was then advertised, that as the expense of producing 1 oz. of gold would cost double the value of the produce, the company would be dissolved, and the deposits kept to pay expenses.

An office was taken and a new company announced with a grand title. The rush for shares was enormous, the issue being subscribed for many times over. Next day an advertisement appeared announcing that the whole concern was a joke to see how many fools could be caught in one day, and the applicants would have their money returned on application.

THE STAG.

A NEW READING FROM "AS YOU LIKE IT."

SCENE—*The Alley.*   *Present—Two Directors.*

1st Dir. Come, shall we take a look at Capel Court?
And yet I'm sorry, when I see the stags,
To think how we, being as bad ourselves,
Do call them rogues and knaves.
    2nd Dir.   Indeed, my friend,
The many-sided Brougham doth grieve at that,
And in that point swears we are more to blame
Than are the rascals that have gammoned us.
To-day, another gentl'man and myself
Did sit beside him, as he took his lunch
In a steak-house, whose antique sign peeps out
Of a dark court, not far from the Exchange.
To which place a poor sequestered stag,
That from a fall in shares had ta'en a hurt,
Did come to languish; and, indeed, my friend,
The wretched animal heaved forth such groans,
That their discharge annoyed the diners round
Almost to cursing; and the big, round tears
Coursed one another down his innocent nose
Into his stout; and thus the hapless stag,
Much marked of the many-sided Brougham,
Sat o'er the poor remains of a small steak,
Moistening his plate with tears.
    1st Dir.   But what said Brougham?
Did he not moralise this spectacle?
    2nd Dir. Oh, yes! into a thousand similes.
First, for his weeping in his needless stout;
"Poor stag," quoth he, "thou makest half-and-half
As tapsters do, putting more water in
To that which had too much." Then, being alone,

HOUSE SCRAPS.

Cleaned out, forsaken by his moneyed friends,
"'Tis right," quoth he, "I foresaw what would come
Of joint-stock companies."—Anon, a lot,
Who'd sold in time, sat down hard by to dine,
And ne'er asked him to join 'em. "Ay," quoth Brougham,
"Dine on, ye fat and greasy citizens;
Had all their rights, you'd be in the same boat
As that decayed and broken bankrupt there."
Thus most invectively he pierceth thro'
The Stock Exchange, the City, Capel Court,
Yea, and Directors; swearing that we, too,
Are men of straw, humbugs, and something worse,
To fall foul of the stags, and drive them out
Of their assigned and native dwelling place.
The Comic Almanack, 1846.

During the mania of 1845 a company was announced, without name, no particulars being given beyond the statement that the most sanguine would be surprised, as the profits were sure to be so enormous. Many rash investors wrote for shares. The promoter and the application-money have not yet been discovered.

ORIGIN OF "HOUSE" FOR THE STOCK EXCHANGE.

The probable origin of the word "House," as applied to the Stock Exchange, is as follows :—Previous to 1801, when the jobbers and brokers (in Government Securities only) assembled, for a short period, in the Rotunda of the Bank of England, a room was rented in a house facing Bartholomew Lane ; when a member was not to be found in the Rotunda it was said: " He is over at the 'House.'" At a later period, when the members moved into their own building, "House" had become a recognised term, which has continued in use until the present day.

It has been suggested that the brokers of Change Alley used the word House as short for coffee-house. I think it will be found that the coffee-houses were always spoken of after the name of the proprietor, as "Jonathan's," "Garraway's," etc.

CHAMPIONS.

The House has always been noted for champions of all sorts of sports and pastimes. Among past or present champions there are—
H. F. Lawford.—Lawn Tennis, 1887.
Geo. Lacy Hillier.—Champion Cyclist at all distances, 1881.
Fred. M. Hobday.—Boxer, 1881.
Schlotel.—Swimmer.
James Paine.—Champion Sculler, 1857.
Playford.—Sculler.
H. J. Chinnery.—Boxer, 1867-71.
H. J. Giles.—Boxer, 1875.

THE STAG, THE BULL, AND THE BEAR
(A Railway Fable.)

THE STAG, THE BULL, AND THE BEAR.

A Railway Fable.

A Stag there was—as I've heard tell,
Who in an attic us'd to dwell,
Or rather—to use a fitter phrase—
Who in an attic used to gaze;
And being blest, like many I know,
With little Conscience, and less Rhino,
Took to that frailest of all frail ways,
And wrote for shares in all the railways;
Applied without the least compunction,
For seventy-five in each new "Junction,"
And gen'rally—the more's the pity—
Got thirty shares from each Committee,
Whereof though it for sale was *not* meant,
He sold the Letter of Allotment.
But this he did, forsooth, because it
Said something rude about Deposit.
    Now he'd applied, and—what was better—
This Stag had just received a letter,
Allotting him some shares, then far
Above the Railway Zero—" par."
" How kind of them," says he, "to gi'e me 'em,
Since they're at such a whacking premium!
'Tis to my soul 'a flatt'ring unction,'
Oh! good St. James's and St. Giles's Junction."
And then the Stag went cap'ring down,
Like many another " buck on town,"
To where " the common herd " resort,
The stony field hight Capel Court,
To where the half-starved *hinds* are seen,
Trying *to nibble all the* " Green."
    But soon to this fam'd cervine quarter
There came a Bull intent on slaughter,
And finding that the Stag I tell of
Had got some shares which were thought well of,
The Bull began to run them down,
And swore they weren't worth half-a-crown;
He call'd it all the worst of names,
This Junction of St. Giles and James;
And thus—these Bulls have so much art with 'em—
At last he got the Stag to part with 'em;
For 'tis with these same Bulls on 'Change
As 'tis with those that meadows range;

To both alike this rule applies,
What they run after's sure to rise.
 Then, wand'ring from his gloomy lair,
In Copthall Court, there came a Bear:
One of that curs'd unfriendly race
Who crush whatever they embrace;
Whose grip is such, whate'er they maul
Is generally sure to fall.
And when he heard the Stag declare
He'd parted with his ev'ry share,
He vow'd the Bull had sorely treated him,
Nay—more he'd say—the Bull had cheated him.
It was the noblest of all schemes,
This Junction of St. Giles and *Jeames!*
However, as he hated knavery,
To do him an especial favour, he
Would let the Stag have thirty more,
At what he sold the others for;
The Stag of gratitude discoursèd,
And took 'em on the terms aforesaid.
 Now all this kindness, from the Bear,
Was nothing but a *"ruse de guerre;"*
For no one knew so well as Bruin
To hold the shares was perfect ruin;
The whole affair was but a swindle,
And down to discount soon would dwindle.
 And, truth to say, the Bear was right,
The panic came like Lillywhite,
That terror of the Lords, and bowl'd out
Every man Jack who had'nt sold out;
So that there was on "settling day,"
The Devil and the Bear to pay.
"But," says the Stag, "that cunning buffer,
The Bull will be the chap to suffer;
So in a cab to him I'll dash up,
And get my taurine friend to cash up."
But when he gets to Mr. Taurus's,
Pasted upon the outer door, he sees
A card with these words written over,
"Gone to Boulogne, *viâ* Dover."
 Now as the Bull had run away,
Unable for the shares to pay,
'Twas clear, as he'd no cash to spare,
The Stag then couldn't pay the Bear;
So when the Bear went for his due,
The Stag had gone to Boulogne too.

And, since the Stag had cut and run,
'Twas plain the Bear could pay no one;
So those to whom he money ow'd,
When they sought out the brute's abode,
Found that the Bear, or him they call so,
Had cut and run to Boulogne also.

MORAL.

Pursue the paths of virtue, and such stale ways,
And don't never have nothing to do with none of those bothering railways.

From *The Comic Almanack*, 1847.

WAITERS?

The origin of naming the attendants, waiters, is not quite clear. They are *not* waiters, nor beadles, nor yet porters. Door-keepers or callers would be more suitable appellatives. It seems almost certain that the name descended from the coffee-house waiters at Jonathan's and elsewhere. When the original House was first opened only two or three door-keepers were engaged. These used to stand outside the door, and come inside to call a member when wanted. They were nearly always addressed by *name* when spoken to by the members. Probably the word came into use naturally as the number of members and waiters increased. "Waiter" sounds more aristocratic than "Porter."

THE SOUTH-SEA BUBBLE

of 1720 created an enormous amount of misery to the holders of the stock when the crash came. The Marquis of Chandos embarked £300,000 in it, and the Duke of Newcastle advised him to sell when he could make a clear profit of 100 per cent. The marquis was anxious to clear half-a-million, and would not sell. The panic came, and every penny was lost.

The elder Scraggs gave Gay £1,000 stock, and as the poet had been a previous purchaser, his gain at one time amounted to £20,000. He consulted Dr. Arbuthnot, who strongly advised him to sell out. The bard doubted, hesitated, and lost all.

Dr. Arbuthnot himself had £2,000 in the same project, and failed to back up his opinion by selling his own stock. The £2,000 was lost, but the doctor comforted himself by saying, it would be only 2,000 pairs of stairs more to ascend.

One investor came to London to sell his holding at 1,000 per cent. On his arrival it had fallen to 900, and as he had decided to sell at 1,000, he determined to wait. The stock continued to decline, the investor continued to hold, and became, as he deserved, a ruined man.

Thomas Guy, the founder of Guy's Hospital, was a large holder of the stock. He sold in time and added a large sum to his already enormous fortune. He left £240,000 to his hospital, and died worth about double that amount.

The poet Gay, writing to his friend Snow, the goldsmith and banker, near Temple Bar, who had been caught by the South-Sea Bubble, says:—

> "Why did 'Change Alley waste thy precious hours
> Among the fools who gaped for golden show'rs?
> No wonder if we found some poets there,
> Who live on fancy and can feed on air;
> No wonder they were caught by South-Sea schemes,
> Who ne'er enjoyed a guinea but in dreams."

Gnats on the Thames.—*1876*.

SCENE.—*Hercules Passage, on a dull afternoon, about* 4.15 *p.m.*
Itinerant vendor of matches (eagerly, to member going home). "I say, sir! is this a 'arfe-past-four-day?"

A jobber, having lost the whole of his fortune, wandered one dark night over London Bridge. He threw his last copper into the flowing stream and was about to follow, when a stranger touched his arm and inquired his reason for wishing to destroy himself. Having learnt the misfortunes of the jobber, the stranger told him some very important information from the Continent (from whence he had just come). Next day the jobber went to the House and bought all the stock he could. Soon after, the news becoming public, a general rise took place. The jobber made enough to pay all his debts, and retired with £20,000.

AN IMPORTANT EVENT.

On Monday, 2nd March, 1885, H.R.H. the Prince of Wales paid a visit to the House. It was the Prince's intention to visit the House *incognito*. This, of course, was found to be impossible. The Prince was received with a tremendous burst of cheering, which lasted until he reached a dais in the south alcove of the new building. The "National Anthem" and "God Bless the Prince of Wales" were sung by the members; a few members of the Stock Exchange Orchestral Society helped to increase the effect. More cheers were then given. The Prince walked round the House and took his departure by the Capel Court door. Later in the day the following telegram was received:—

To the Chairman, etc. etc., of the Stock Exchange.

MARLBOROUGH HOUSE, PALL MALL, S.W.,
2nd March, 1885.

DEAR SIR,—I am desired by the Prince of Wales to convey, through you, to the members of the Stock Exchange, the expression of his very cordial thanks for the loyal and hearty welcome they gave him this morning. The welcome which his Royal Highness met with has never been surpassed, and I am directed to assure you that he derived the highest gratification from his most interesting visit.—I beg to remain, &c.,

(Signed) FRANCIS KNOLLYS.

PAPER-CREDIT.

Blest paper-credit! last and best supply!
That lends Corruption lighter wings to fly!
Gold imp'd by thee can compass hardest things—
Can pocket States, can fetch or carry Kings;
A single leaf shall waft an Army o'er,
Or ship off Senates to a distant Shore;
A leaf, like Sibyl's, scatter to and fro
Our fates and fortunes, as the winds shall blow:
Pregnant with thousands flits the Scrap unseen,
And silent sells a King, or buys a Queen.

Pope's Moral Essays.

ROBBED!

A lady bought £3,000 Unified. They were delivered in £20 bonds, and safely deposited at the National Safe Deposit Company in a box shared with her husband. The latter, finding they took up a lot of room, changed them for three bonds of £1,000. Soon afterwards the wife went to the City to cut off the coupons, and was horrified to find "all the bonds stolen but three." After threatening to bring an action against the company, and having a general row, she took the three coupons to her broker. He was able to explain the matter, but the shock of (as she thought) finding herself robbed was very great, and upset her for some days.

OUR ADVERTISERS.

Stock-Jobbing, Speculative, Financial, &c.

SQUARUM SHARPE, STOCK AND SHARE BROKER.

SQUARUM SHARPE'S WEST BROMPTON AND MILE END EXCHANGES.

SQUARUM SHARPE is prepared to open accounts, with or without cover, with everybody and anybody, on the slightest provocation.

UNSUSPECTING CLERGYMEN, CONFIDING WIDOWS, and SPECULATIVE HALF-PAY OFFICERS are invited to inspect SQUARUM SHARPE'S SELF-SUPPORTING INVESTMENT CIRCULAR, which will show them at a glance how, with a little ready money, they can, with unbounded confidence, dispose of it irrevocably to somebody's immediate advantage, and in fact enable a more fortunate "Operator" to realise

EVEN IN ONE AFTERNOON all the advantages of A COLOSSAL FORTUNE.

SQUARUM SHARPE, Stockbroker.

GOLIGHTLY BROTHERS, Stock Brokers,

BUY OR SELL with an inclusive Commission of 1—26th, and open any Stock, no matter how shaky, on receipt of ¼ per cent. cover.

GOLIGHTLY BROTHERS have just inaugurated their new West End and City Offices, that have been arranged so that they will be found replete with every convenience and allurement for the Intending Operator. Forty separate rooms furnished with Superior Lounges, approached by Lifts, and supplied with all the leading Stock and Share Journals in the United Kingdom. A staff of polished and experienced Clerks, who have special facilities for acquiring information as to the fluctuation of the Money Market from a Cabinet Minister kept permanently on the premises for the purpose, are in continual attendance to give advice to Speculators. Champagne on the premises for the convenience of Country Customers. Tape laid on to any distance, in any quantity.

GOLIGHTLY BROTHERS will be pleased to forward, gratis, their Opinion on the probable movements of the Mexican Market to anyone who will read it.

THERE IS NOW A STOCK that should be utilized for the purpose of taking immediate advantage of the public, who will be induced to hope to get out of it handsome profits. Messrs. GOLIGHTLY have been studying this stock, and the more they look at it the more they like it, and so they

---

JERRYWEATHER & CO., large-hearted and philanthropic Stock and Share Brokers.

JERRYWEATHER & CO., though they have never operated with a less profit on the month's transactions than 195 per cent., have no wish to keep the benefit of their successful negotiations for themselves, but are anxious, on the contrary, to secure this handsome profit solely for the good of their clients.

JERRYWEATHER & CO. are contented therefore to pocket a mere nominal commission, together with the amount of cover on each operation.

JERRYWEATHER & CO., large-hearted and philanthropic Stock and Share Brokers.

JERRYWEATHER & CO. have hundreds of testimonials from Peers of the Realm, Archbishops, Members of Parliament, and Professional Celebrities, heartily thanking them for their disinterested financial aid and assistance, and they strongly advise their intending clients not to wait, but to forward their cheques for cover from £10 to £500 without delay, when they will forthwith commence operations on their behalf.

JERRYWEATHER & CO. submit extract from *Civil Service Chronicle*:—"Those who wish to part quietly with their money cannot do better than entrust it to the judicious manipulation of Messrs. JERRYWEATHER."

able to operate to their advantage. That enormous fortunes have been made by simply watching the movements of one Stock is testified to by the fact that a real live Nobleman, who has retired in consequence of a successful operation in this direction, is to be seen any day at their offices, happy to furnish chapter and verse, to vouch for the truth of his experiences.

GOLIGHTLY BROTHERS advised purchase of New Granada Cents, at 69½. They have since been as low as 32, showing a loss of £396, including a cover of £15.

GOLIGHTLY BROTHERS advised purchase of South Pacifics at 72½. They are now quoted at 16, involving a loss of £427, together with a cover of £20.

GOLIGHTLY BROTHERS, STOCK BROKERS.

PACKWELL'S SYNDICATES.

THESE REMARKABLE INVESTMENTS, worked on an entirely new plan, continue to give unbounded satisfaction and surprise to hopeful subscribers.

IT IS CALCULATED that not less than 475 per cent. profit upon the capital invested will be realised, so that

£5 will command £700
10   „   „   1,400
50   „   „   7,000
100 „   „   14,000

THESE FIGURES, which will soon be verified by a reference to our books, speak for themselves, and serve to show intending Customers how carefully their interests will be guarded by Messrs. PACKWELL. Shares must be paid for in full on application.

PACKWELL'S SYNDICATES.

of Mr. SHARPE's method of proceeding, and can only describe it as marvellously ingenious. By a judicious insertion of advertisement he attracts a certain number of confiding country and other clients, who, greedy of realising fictitious profits themselves, hand over to him their cheques for a one or two per cent. 'cover,' as the case may be. There is a fall in the special Stock or Stocks 'operated upon,' and the result is that the cover at once disappears, and in a short time, though their places are soon filled by other eager votaries, Mr. SHARPE's confiding country clients as well."

MONACOS. — SQUARUM SHARPE has confidently recommended a plunge into these elastic securities for the fall with the best results. His clients have been fairly warned off them for good.

SQUARUM SHARPE points out that his system of operating on his clients has been pursued by him with the greatest success, a success which dozens of threatening letters received by him daily, and that can be seen at his office, corroborate and establish.

SQUARUM SHARPE does not recommend caution.

SQUARUM SHARPE does not advise circumspection.

SQUARUM SHARPE counsels all his clients to treat Investment as if it were nothing more or less than

A GAME OF BLIND HOOKEY.

SOUNDER ADVICE than this was never given to fluttering operators. SQUARUM SHARPE does not undertake to guarantee a surprise in every transaction, but we may safely predict that a strict adherence to his methods and advice will, in the long run, lead the speculator to experience astonishment and even amazement.

FRANK GRABBINGTON'S New and Unique System of rapidly acquiring a Large Fortune.

FRANK GRABBINGTON'S Discretionary Investment Circular should be read by hesitating Operators. He says:

OWING TO EXCEPTIONAL ADVANTAGES I enjoy of being behind the Ministerial scenes, and having direct telephonic communication with the leading Statesmen of Europe, I am in a position to advise my clients in the selection of such Central American Stocks, the slightest movement of which will fairly startle them.

OPTIONS. I do not recommend these. Experience has proved that when Clients have no option whatever in the matter of Investment, the highest and most surprising results are invariably achieved.

REALISING. — Clients should not allow themselves to be deterred from further speculation by realising thoroughly how they have been already done. I strongly advise against this.

FRANK GRABBINGTON receives Stocks, Scrip, Coupons, Cheques, Ready Money, and Postage Stamps, or anything negotiable, and is prepared to deal with them, or with any of his country Clients by telegraph, or attend them at their own residences at tape prices.

FRANK GRABBINGTON'S Discretionary Investment Circular. The Bloomsbury Mercantile Exchange says of it:— "We can conceive no readier method of enabling nervous speculators to divest themselves of their little savings, than by taking the Discretionary plunge recommended by this artful paper. Mr. FRANK GRABBINGTON is evidently determined not to be outdone by his compeers."

A FEW CELEBRATED HOAXES.

The first political hoax on record occurred in the reign of Anne. Down the Queen's Road, riding at a furious rate, ordering turnpikes to be thrown open, and loudly proclaiming the sudden death of the Queen, rode a well-dressed man, sparing neither spur nor steed. From west to east, and from north to south, the news spread. Like wildfire it passed through the desolate fields where palaces now abound, till it reached the City. The train bands desisted from their exercise, furled their colours, and returned home with their arms reversed. The funds fell with a suddenness which marked the importance of the intelligence; and it was remarked that, while the Christian jobbers stood aloof, almost paralyzed with the information, Manasseh Lopez and the Jew interest bought eagerly at the reduced price. There is no positive information to fix the deception upon anyone in particular, but suspicion was pointed at those who gained by the fraud so publicly perpetrated.

On the 5th May, 1803, the following letter was posted upon a board conspicuously displayed outside the Mansion House, usually allotted for posting important information:—

"Lord Hawkesbury presents his compliments to the Lord Mayor, and has the honour to acquaint his lordship that the negociation between this country and the French Republic is brought to an amicable conclusion."

The glad tidings soon reached the Stock Exchange; the funds rose from 63 to 70. This pleasant state of affairs did not continue for long. Suspicion was aroused; men doubted, though they scarcely knew why. Consols fluctuated, with a downward tendency, and great uneasiness prevailed. Amid a confusion, an uproar, and a noise, at that period unprecedented, the Lord Mayor read the contents of a second letter. Business was immediately suspended, and all bargains were declared void. The projectors of this hoax were never discovered.

Again, in May, 1832, a run upon the Bank of England was produced by the walls of London being placarded with the emphatic words, "To stop the Duke, go for gold"—advice which was followed, as soon as given, to a prodigious extent. The Duke of Wellington was then very unpopular; and on Monday, the 14th of May, it being currently believed that the Duke had formed a cabinet, the panic became universal. The idea of the placards originated with four gentlemen: each put down £20, and the total sum was used in printing thousands of these terrible missives. The effect is hardly to be described. It was electric.

Most of our readers will remember the hoax in Peruvians which occurred about three years ago, when a letter was received by the secretary of the Stock Exchange purporting to come from Mr. Gladstone's private secretary, and stating that negotiations had been successfully arranged with the Chilian Government respecting the claims of the Peruvian Bondholders. No sooner was the letter containing this unexpected news posted on one of the notice boards, than Perus began to rise, and in the space of a few minutes showed an advance of 5 or 6 per cent. But the rise was of short duration; men began to doubt the truth of the information, and pointed out that such a communication would naturally have come from the Foreign Office, and not from Mr. Gladstone. On enquiry it was discovered the whole affair was a fraud; the letter (which, by-the-bye, was on official paper) was promptly taken down, and Peruvians dropped to their former figure with the same celerity with which they had risen. Although the Committee did all in their power to ascertain the writer of the letter, nothing, we believe, was ever discovered.

A DIALOGUE.

A. "What a waste of energy has been C——'s life! He has made a fortune, it's true, but he has done no good with it, and when he dies he cannot take it with him."

B. "That's well, perhaps, for him, for if he could there's little doubt he'd soon see it *melt*."

HOW THEY DIDN'T MANAGE THESE THINGS BETTER IN FRANCE.

At the time of our South-Sea mania France was provided with an identical folly in Law's scheme for colonising in Mississippi. The scene of all the transactions in the shares of his scheme was the Rue Quincampoix, a Parisian 'Change Alley. In the "Mémoires du Cardinal Dubois" it is described as being long, narrow, and very dirty. The inhabitants were practically prisoners in their own houses all the day, or, if they got out before the crowds began to collect early in the morning, there was no chance of returning to their homes till it dispersed at night. The bursting of the French bubble actually contributed to give the *coup-de-grâce* to our South-Sea one.

One of the episodes of it is the fortune that is said to have been made by a little humpback, who, by means of his hump, let himself out as a peripatetic desk on which the various kinds of writing the circumstances required could be done. In the dense throng which prevailed the whole day long this must have been an advantage that everyone competed for. What a mass they formed can be estimated by the fact that the privileges of the highest rank were there utterly effaced. The Dowager Princess of Conti endeavoured, on one occasion, to drive into the street, even at the risk of running over everyone who got in the way; but the officials appointed to regulate the traffic at once had the carriage stopped. She let them know she was the Princess of Conti. "Were you the Princess of Mississippi," was the immediate rejoinder, "you should not move an inch." The sole nobility there were the successful speculators. Society, for the time being, was all at sixes and sevens. Dubois has one story to tell of one of his valets, whom he got rid of because he was so deficient in diligence when dispatched on any errand. He met him, he says, shortly after getting rid of him, so stylishly dressed and riding in such a splendid carriage, that he would have utterly failed to identify him had not the saucy fellow said, "Ah! Monseigneur, I am a better runner than you took me for; I have run in pursuit of Fortune, and succeeded, too, in catching her."

Fontenelle relates a comical story of another, a coachman, who, for some time before he got fully accustomed to a carriage of his own, which he was able to start by his luck in speculation, used, now and then, mechanically jump up behind it. This has somewhat of a parallel in the case of the nobleman whose coachman, for similar reasons, gave him sudden notice of his intention to leave his service. All the master could do was to get the man's promise that he would find a substitute the next day. He appeared with a couple. "But," said his employer, "I want only one." "Right enough," was the retort, "but I mean to retain the other for my own service."

A witty workman has the credit of having exclaimed, on seeing a very vulgar but brilliantly be-jewelled woman step from a carriage—"This Princess must have fallen from a garret window, and had her fall broken by the carriage passing below just at the right moment."

A Madame Bezon was one evening at the opera with her daughter, when she had her attention drawn to a neighbouring box by the ostentatious entrance into it of a very stout woman, dressed in most glaring colours, and all brilliant with gold and silver ornaments. Before her daughter could recover her surprise she exclaimed, "Why, it's our cook, Marie!" "Be quiet, dear," was Madame Bezon's reply; "you will expose us to a shower of abuse." By this time, however, the attention of the whole house was drawn to their direction. All over it was heard—"There's Marie, the cook!" Other pleasantries followed so fast and thick that the be-dressed and be-jewelled woman, unable any longer to control her rising anger, burst out with the following speech:—"I don't deny that I was your cook, and a very good cook too; but I am a millionaire now. I have made a fortune in the Rue Quincampoix, and mean to enjoy it. I spend some in fine dresses, and what is more, pay for them—which you can't always say, Madame Bezon, for you are in my debt for a part of my wages!" The immediate effect was the retirement of Madame Bezon, and the cook, left mistress of the field, sat down, proudly enjoying the effect of the scene upon the now sympathetic audience.

The following is one of the many epigrams with which the occasion was ripe:—

> Qui l'aurait cru ? miracle étrange!
> Aujourd'hui par les soins de Law,
> Comme dans les mains de Midas,
> Dans nos mains tout en or se change!
> Que chacun prenne garde à soi :
> Après avoir chanté merveilles,
> Il pourrait bien, comme à ce roi,
> Nous venir de grandes oreilles.

HOUSE SCRAPS.

The double allusion herein made to the property conferred by the gods, at his own solicitation, upon the hands of Midas, of turning all they touched to gold, and to the other legend of his long, ass-like ears, which he fruitlessly took such precautions to hide, gives it a two-fold barb. As a loose paraphrase, the following may not be unwelcome:—

> Our hands, like those of Midas, king of old,
> Law helps to turn whate'er they touch to gold;
> Like Midas, too, there's room to fear
> We may be famous for our length of ear.

One of Law's favourite diversions was to fling handfuls of gold from a window of one of the houses in the Rue Quincampoix, and enjoy the sight of the mass below scrambling and fighting among themselves for the pieces.

TUMBLING OUT ON A { LION LYING } RUMOUR.

The following epigram was stuck on a notice of the Stock Exchange Christian Association, 21st October, 1887. Mr. A. H. Sly, Hon. Sec., and Mr. A. Ballance, Treasurer.

> "There may be some who'd fain descry
> Danger in our Secretary being *Sly;*
> But let them, this once, spare their talents,
> Our Treasury means to keep its *Ballance.*"

Some years ago a member complained of not having had any sleep on account of a dance one side of his house and the sweep on the other. The following was written at the time, under a caricature:—

> "Poor Mr. Ted he went to bed,
> But could not get to sleep,
> For the dance next door went on till four,
> And at five there came the sweep."

> There ain't no H in 'Ouse,
> There ain't no H at all;
> There ain't no H in 'Enery,
> Nor yet in 'Arry 'All.

THE MANSION HOUSE BANQUET:

A STOCK EXCHANGE BALLAD.

Good people all, to live who seek
    Upon the Stock Exchange;
Of your Committee hear me speak,
    And their adventures strange.

How that it happened on a day,
    Lord Mayor asked them to dine;
And how they went in brave array
    Of broadcloth superfine.

You mostly see them poorly dressed;
    You seem to hold them small;
But had you met them in their best,
    You must have loved them all.

My friends, it was a gallant sight,
    As up the stairs they came:
In patent boots, and chokers white,
    And were called out by name.

The great Lord Mayor, to greet each friend,
    Within his Hall did stand;
Search England through from end to end,
    There nothing is so grand.

For sinister, one held a mace;
    Dexter, a sword did bear;
An awful cap hid Dexter's face,
    Made out of tom cats' hair.

In velvet suit, and baggy wig,
    With sword upon the thigh,
Two Sheriffs stood: one very big,
    The other five feet high.

Your first, that goodly cheer to seek,
    Was Ingall, known to all;
Bystanders whispered: "For a week
    He has not dined at all."

Then soon came Scrutton the severe,
    Scott, Gibbs, and Spurling bald;
Dramatic Slous, Tom Fenn were there,
    And Smith of Grisewood called.

Too fast to hear, next, in a row,
   Came names of worthies pleasant;
But you will all be glad to know,
   That Mister Pearce was present.

Stayed for a moment was the tide
   Of men, and all was still,
Until the crier gently sighed,
   The name of Umbleville.

Then cheek by jowl, and all for love,
   Your Chairman's presence seeking,
Were shouted out, all noise above,
   Strawbridge, and Roger Eykyn.

Last man, appeared your Chairman good,
   Your mind I would not shock it;
But as before Lord Mayor he stood,
   His hand was in his pocket.

"Dinner is served, Lord Mayor!" they cried,
   Then proudly did we see,
That seated by his Lordship's side,
   Your Chairman was to be.

Oh, then came feasting fast and high,
   Soup, fish, and dainties fine,
Game, jellies, ices, apple pie,
   And every kind of wine.

Your senators are counted staid,
   But had you seen them then,
With winks, and jokes, and "Who's afraid?"
   They were quite other men.

At last the dinner it was done,
   His Lordship he stood up,
And kindly pledged to every one
   Health in the loving cup.

He gave the Queen, our warriors brave,
   Then ventured to advance,
That if the public specs will have,
   They never stand a chance.

And then he called for, pleasantly,
   To me it sounded strange—
We meet with so much calumny—
   Health to the Stock Exchange.

Your Chairman apt, accepts the fun,
    And takes on him to say:
Clients are not by brokers done—
    It is the other way.

Money by some is held to be
    An agent of the devil,
But granting money, Banks, and we
    Are necessary evil.

They cheered him—he had made a hit—
    His Lordship laughed right hearty:
And then the singers sang a bit:
    It was a pleasant party.

At last your Chairman asked Lord Mayor
    A not quite proper riddle,
Which caused him to vacate the chair,
    Nor stay to hear a fiddle.

Oh, then outcame your Chairman bold,
    Close followed by his Vice,
Baker, and Wedd, and Flower old,
    And stalwart Rokeby Price.

Alas! What different men came out
    To those who went inside:
Noses were red, hair tossed about,
    And eyes they multiplied.

They had walked in, each one by one,
    A steady, even pace;
Now out, by two and two, they run,
    As in a three-legged race.

Their gibus hats are cocked awry,
    Untied their chokers white;
As, maudlin in their melody,
    They sing "Lord Mayor, good night."

Strong wine, it is a potent thing,
    While human brains are weak;
So Bacchus always tries to sing
    When he no more can speak.

Still all is well that well doth end,
    Singly they ill had sped;
But every man held up his friend
    So all got safe to bed.

HOUSE SCRAPS. 145

God save her gracious Majesty—
Her enemies cast down;
And may the Stock Exchange e'er be
True subjects to the Crown.

Good luck and great prosperity
Alight on Lord Mayor Cotton,
And by Lord Mayors to come may we
Henceforth be not forgotten.

Good luck to our Committee, too—
May they live soberly;
And when such valiant deeds they do,
May I be there to see.

[The above refers to the occasion when Lord Mayor Cotton invited the Managers and Committee of the Stock Exchange to meet the Directors and Managers of some of the Banks and Insurance Companies. This poem, written by P—— S——, was sold for the benefit of the Benevolent Fund, and realised about £8.]

REMARKABLE FISH LATELY SEEN OFF THE COAST OF SCOTLAND, NEAR THE FRITH, SUPPOSED TO BE A NEW VARIETY OF THE ODD FISH.—*1876.*

A diabolical policy has been handed about in the City, giving five guineas, to return one hundred, if the three ambassador's heads, at Constantinople, were off on the 15th November.—*Globe*, 1827.

L

GUY FAWKES AT THE STOCK EXCHANGE.

During the whole of Monday the Stock Exchange was the scene of smoke and bustle, occasioned by the discharge of squibs, crackers, and catherine-wheels. A considerable sum was raised for the purchase of the fireworks, by the following ingenious method:—About half-a-dozen of the members went round "the House" with a well-written petition, to receive subscriptions for Mrs. Fawkes, a widow with a large family, in great distress. Many gave their shillings and half-crowns, and upwards of £12 were collected. No idea was entertained of the hoax until Saturday, when the following announcement was placarded—"The Committee appointed to manage the subscription for the widow Fawkes and family, will make a *report* on Monday next." A wag remarked, "That this was not the only affair emanating from the Stock Exchange which ended in *smoke*."—*Examiner*, November 11th, 1827.

A marine insurance company at Cadiz once took the Virgin Mary into formal partnership, covenanting to set aside her portion of profits for the enrichment of her shrine in that city. Not doubting that she would protect every vessel in which she had such a manifest interest, they underwrote ships of all sorts at such reduced rates that in a few months the partners were all declared bankrupts—which proves that the Blessed Virgin was no friend to joint-stock companies.—*Examiner*, 1827.

SEATS IN THE STOCK EXCHANGE.

The sum of $30,000 was recently paid as the price of a transferred share and seat in the New York Stock Exchange, together with $1,000 fees of transfer. The stockholders, in November, 1879, increased the membership from 1,060 to 1,100, and the initiation fee from $10,000 to $20,000 after the additional forty members had joined—although it is an unwritten law of the Exchange that the last limit authorised shall not be exceeded. The funds thus raised—$400,000—went to the building account, and the limit of membership having been substantially reached, $20,000 has been the par price of seats for more than a year past, although premiums of $3,000 or $5,000 have been paid. It is prophesied that before many years seats will be sold at $100,000. This sum, large as it seems, will not equal the prices which have been paid on the Paris Bourse for the place of one of the sixty Agents de Change appointed by the Government. These places of late years have fluctuated from $300,000 to $500,000 in our money. But when we consider that there are but sixty such places in Paris, against more than a thousand here, the present and prospective value of New York Stock Exchange privileges will appear to be far the greater of the two. Members of the London Stock Exchange pay an initiation fee of $750 in our money and about $100 yearly dues.—From *Frank Leslie's Illustrated Newspaper*, of February 12th, 1881.

GAMBLING WOMEN.

How many greedy, gambling women are there in England? Not only in and about the Wen, but in every country town, in every village you will find them, to gamble in funds or shares of some sort or other; and who cannot sit with you five minutes without your hearing some of their slang about fives and fours and threes, and consols and reduceds and India and Greek, and so on. A woman asked me my opinion one day about *investing*, as she called it, some money that she had. She had got some fours and some threes, and something else, and she wanted to know if there was no other good thing that she could get. I make free, as to giving men advice, now and then; but experience has taught me to be very careful how I presume, in this way, with petticoat speculators. Being pressed, however, with some degree of earnestness, I advised the getting rid of all the securities of every sort, and took an opportunity of showing, very clearly, as I thought, how much more secure, as well as more honourable, the possession of land or house, or security on land or house, would be than the possession of a thing that may become of no value at all to-morrow; adding some observations on the lowness, the meanness, the filthiness of these sort of usurious transactions, appealing, by a side wind, to her religion, of which she professed to have a pretty large quantity, which she discovered by crying, "Oh, fye!" when I d——d all the funds. In short, I, before I concluded, had made, as I thought, great impression on her mind, if I had not already converted her. After this, a short pause ensued, while we were looking out of the window, and I was admiring some very pretty rose trees. And she, all at once, as if I had never said a word to her upon the subject of funds and bonds, asked me, with great seeming earnestness, "Mr. Cobbett, *what do you think of Colombian?*" I know what I thought of her, though I did not tell her; and that was, that she was a nasty, gambling, grovelling, mercenary, sordid, merciless devil in petticoats, who did not care if all the people of the village in which she lived perished with hunger, provided that the cause of that perishing were also the cause of making her gain, however unjustly and basely, a few additional pounds a year. A man that is a stock jobber is bad enough—he is wretch enough; but a woman that is a stock jobber is, according to the ordinary proportions of good and evil in the two sexes, beyond all measure worse. As women are better than men in good qualities, they are worse in bad qualities. A stock-jobbing man is the worst of men, and a stock-jobbing woman is fit for Lucifer's wife.—*Cobbett's Register*, 1827.

A member once asked Mr. T—— for a $\frac{1}{16}$ price in Consols, and was told to "go to the Devil." The following was posted in the market:—

> "Mr. T——, in language more potent than civil,
> Told Charles Henry A—ton to go to the Devil.
> He staggered away with bouncing bravado,
> And not finding Koser he dealt with Mikado."

WIT.

Amid all the varieties of "House" wit, I have not heard of any display of it at any festivities in connection with, say, its Benevolent Fund. Should any member aspire to enliven a future gathering of this sort of his fellow members, the following story may serve for a pattern. It happened at a Benchers' banquet, given to congratulate Shee and Lush on their elevation to the Bench:—"Gentlemen," said the Chairman, "I have to propose some modification in one of our customary toasts. In lieu of the usual 'Wine and Woman,' I beg to substitute 'Lush and Shee.'"

CAUSE AND EFFECT.

It is said that Mabey's barmaids always know how the markets are going. When things are very dull and markets are tumbling to pieces, a greater number of "nips" are taken, spirits being in great demand. On the other hand, when everything is going up, there is a general run on iced drinks, champagne, and other light beverages. They can always palm off a tough steak on a Bull in a rising market; but have to give a Bear something very light under the same circumstances. Bears are bad eaters, even when things are going the right way for them. Bulls eat tarts and buns, Bears drink spirits and leave the pastry alone. A Bull eats his dinner very quickly, whereas a Bear eats slowly and grumbles about everything. Bulls are easily pleased; Bears want a lot of attention. A sharp waiter knows what a customer is, and treats him accordingly.

SOUND INVESTMENTS.

During the excitement over the South-Sea Bubble of 1721, about 150 companies were floated, representing over £300,000,000. All the shares were at a premium of 100 per cent., many 500 per cent., and some even at 1,000 per cent. The following are selected as specimens:—

The Company for a flying machine.
,, ,, curing the gout and stone.
,, ,, an air-pump for the brain.
,, ,, making butter from beech trees.
,, ,, making radish oil.
,, ,, a perpetual motion.
,, ,, making deal boards from sawdust.
,, ,, an engine to remove South-Sea House into Moorfields.
,, ,, extracting silver from lead.
,, ,, a scheme to learn wise men to cast nativities.

SCENE—*A Hunting Field.*
First Rider. "Who's that just tumbled off?"
Second Rider. "Oh, he's only a stock-broker. He told me he was going for a fall this morning."

HOUSE SCRAPS.

One day a member asked a friend why Consols were good. His friend (rather fond of showing off his French) said, "*Tout le Monde* is buying." The other, not being a scholar, went about and said that the "two Le Mondes were buying." Le Monde Bros. were members.

CUPID, *after* RUBENS.—*March, 1874.*

About 1820 some members issued tokens or medals. I have one issued by John Ashby, Stock Broker, No. 3, Bartholomew Lane, Bank. Above his name is a Bull, on the obverse side is a Bear, and under it the following :—

FIXED HOLIDAYS.

January ...	1, 6, 25, 29, 30	July ...	19, 25
February	2, 24	August ...	... 24
March ...	... 25	September	2, 21, 29
April	23	October ...	... 18, 28
May	1, 29	November	1, 4, 5, 9, 30
June	... 11, 24, 29	December	... 21, 25, 26, 27, 28

Office Hours from 10 to 3.

John Ashby was a member from 1814 to 1834.

A CHAT WITH AN OLD MEMBER.

When I first came here the place was very different from what it is now. We were only a few hundred strong then, and everybody knew everybody else. I think the tone of the business is lower now. Of course, increased competition has had its inevitable effect. We used to deal at wider prices then, and commissions were paid in full. Bucket shops were not even looming in the future. We had some fine games in the old days. At 2, Capel Court, Mendoza had a boxing booth, where, instead of knocking prices about, a member could go and knock somebody about or get knocked about himself, if things did not suit him inside. An old woman had a stall *inside* the House, close to Capel Court door, where those who had not quite outlived their earliest tastes could feed on buns, cakes, etc. She eventually, so it is said, made a small fortune out of the members, and retired from business. She had a moral reason for it too—she said the Stock Exchange "was such a wicked place." A gallery ran round the old House; seats and desks were fitted up for clerks and members. It was very convenient, because if a man wanted a book he simply called up to his clerk, who would throw it over. Some of the funny ones used to drop things over on unsuspecting members. Sometimes, in the afternoon, a jobber used to give us a tune on a cornet, and I reckon we had plenty of fun when things were dull. The whole character of the business has changed since then, and I fancy that if some of the old boys could come back again they would hardly know their own business. We used to buy our own chops and steaks in those days, and take them to a cook-shop or chop-house and have them cooked, paying a penny for the privilege; they furnished the vegetables and drink, bread, etc. That is the origin of all the cooks at the chop-houses expecting a penny in the present day. The modern palatial dining-rooms were not even thought of.

The "Almanack" was about the cleverest thing ever written in the House. Several members had a hand in it. At first, nobody could be got to print it, the printers being afraid of actions for libel. As it happened, it caused much amusement, and, with one exception, no mischief.

Almost over every bargain a glass of sherry used to be drunk. "Who pays?" was a very common expression.

It is said that an old member made use of some very queer expressions. Once he told a youth who had been cheeking him that he was "a *precockious* youth, and would die a *primitive* death." When Consols were going up, and he could not understand why, he said "it was a complete *enema*" to him. When somebody told him of a new invention, he said "it was more *theological* than *pragmatical*."

One morning a member came to the City in a new pair of very baggy homespun trousers. The following was written on the occasion:—

"Fineweather Sheepshanks" rose one day
From an orthodox bed in the orthodox way,
In an orthodox nightshirt's gauzy array;
And leaving his shell with an air *négligé*
    In his tub he proceeded to wallow.
Refreshed, he arose: sought around for his clothes;
And proceeded to dress; but words cannot express
His despairing amazement and abject distress—
    His bewilderment, anger, and sorrow.
His trousers weren't there—not a thing he could wear,
    And devil a pair he could borrow!

What was he to do? There wasn't a doubt—
He'd turned the whole wardrobe three times inside out;
The things WERE NOT there—he could not do without—
    He seized on some brandy and drank it. . .
Who'd got them? His servant? Perhaps up the spout!
His agonised gaze as it wandered about
    Alighted at last on the blanket!
Joy filled his eyes. Here at least was a prize
That would serve for a time a sufficient disguise,
    With the aid of a few hurried stitches:
Rejoiced with the plan that had entered his head,
He rang for some scissors, a needle, and thread,
And within half an hour since he jumped out of bed
    Stood erect in his present new breeches!

TWO CHAMPIONS OF THE "RING."

Jay Gould and Sullivan have reached our shores,
To rest, they say, a little on their oars.
The first, the champion of "the vast Wabash,"
Makes millions when his railroads "go to smash;"
And only wins our confidence to mock it,
And filch our savings from our breeches pocket.
The other—champion of a worthier "ring,"
Where good, fair, stand-up fighting is the thing—
However hard another's blows he felt,
Would scorn, we ween, to hit beneath the belt.
Now, which of these, think you, 's the better man?
We give our vote to J. L. Sullivan.
              Financial News, November 10th, 1887.

A TALE OF THE "STOCK EXCHANGE."

Two **Archers** going round the **Angle** of a **Backhouse** met a **Baillie**, a **Hardy Scott** named **Stuart Tudor**, with some **Bakers** and **Barbers** and a **Batchelor**, who was a **Dandy**, a **Swaine**, a perfect **Bauman** and a **Chalmer**, also a **Wagg**, possessing great **Vertue** riding in three **Barrows**, with four **Butlers** and a **Butcher** who wore a **Belcher** handkerchief and a **Buckler**, they cut a **Bigg Birch**, and made three **Bishops** sign a **Bond**.

They then took the **Carrs West**, and made the **Carter Chalk** some **Cases** of **Bones**, which they took to the **Chandlers' Chambers**, after which they went to **Clapham** and met a **Bland Chancellor**, with a **Chamberlain**, a **Chaplain**, a **Clark**, and a **Child**, and took all their **Coates** and made a **Collier** bring them **Coles** to **Cook** a **Crabb** for their **Cousins**; they then came across a **Cooper** with a piece of **Cork** and some **Craven Crews** who **Daly** went to the **Downes** by the **Dee** to try to catch a **Dolphin**.

Going by **De Pass** to **England**, they saw a **Drake** and **De Wesele** swallowing **De Worms**, and a **Fatt Faulconer Fagg** over a **Fenn** after a **Fox** and a **Gardener** with a **Rose**, and some **Flowers**, looking like **Grimaldi** up to his **Gaimes**, with a **Gray Finch**. Going through the **Greenfields**, and **Greenwoods**, and over the **Greenhills**, they met a **Harper** bidding **Goodday** to a **Guy** in some **Hall** near **Hastings**.

They next went to their **Holmes** in **Holland** to **Hunt** for a **Hatch**, a **Hutt**, and a **Woodhouse**, the **Lack** of which made them **Grieve**. They then came back to **Kent** and took the **Kings** to **Lancaster** in a **Landau**, and **Littlejohn** (**Jacks**) being a **Lightbody**, with them to **Lock** the **Lodge** on the **Marsh** to keep the **Lyon** in, and went into the **Kitchen** to **Burn** some **Wood** to **Fry** a **Pidgeon**, a **Partridge**, and another **Bird** with **Peppercornes**. After this **Medley** they met a **Merchant** and a **Miller** coming **Miles** from his **Mills** over the **Moor** with a **Monk**. And by the **May Moon** they went **Nutting** and got plenty of **Nutts** and some **Oates**, and took them along a **Ridge** up to a **Peake** where they saw a **Pittmann** go into the **Pitts** with a **Pott** of **Porter**.

Prior to this they went over a **Privett** hedge and obtained a **Winch** and a **Pulley** to lower themselves, when one hurt his **Legg**, which gave him great **Paine**, and made them **Sadd**, but they had some **Rolls** and **Salmon** on the **Sly**, and then took their **Shanks** off **Sharp** to **Shadwell** to look after a **Short Sheppard** and a **Shorter Sherreff**, but found some **Squires** wearing **Hood**, **Spencer** and **Tassell**, which they stole, and these being their **Stock** they tried to sell them to the **Taylors** in a **Temple** to make them **Tidy**, but they were **Towgood**, so they **Raphael**'d them.

Lastly, they were brought to **Towne** by a **Constable**, taken before a **Mayor** and put into a **Ward** in **Milbank**.

J. G. B.

CHINESE TURNPIKES.

It has always been considered the proper thing in the House for some trap to be laid for a new jobber, or a jobber starting in a new market. The different bogus companies that have been floated for this purpose are legion. Chinese Turnpike Bonds is about the oldest, and only a month or two ago was resorted to to amuse the jobbers in the miscellaneous market. Nearly everybody knows how the oracle is worked—how the jobbers agree, on a certain day, to start dealing in the bogus concern, a few brokers being let into the secret. The novice is at once taken in, "starts a book," and soon makes, he thinks, "good easy man," a lot of money. Well managed, the joke may last several days. Experienced jobbers of even twenty years' standing have been caught at this game. Some fellows won't bite at first, so bogus telegrams are sent from the country, and other dodges are tried, even to printing a prospectus of the company. In the end, it proves to be a very cruel experience for the member who falls into the trap. Some have been so elated by their luck that they have bought their wives sealskin jackets, etc. In one case a jobber losing, it seemed, a heap of money, almost committed suicide from grief. Another jobber made a large profit, but when he discovered it was all fairy money the shock affected his head, and he never came back to the House. A very cute jobber was once beautifully had over a South American Tramway Company. He got the tip to buy, and therefore "laid in" 300 shares. Only half-a-dozen members were in the secret, which they kept so well that the bogus shares went gradually up during eight or nine days from £4 to £6. The jobber re-sold some of the shares and passed his name for the rest. It was only when the jokers possessed his name that the cat was let out of the bag.

HEAVY FALL IN THE RUBBISH MARKET.

THACKERAY AND HORACE SMITH.

In one of the piquant Collection of his Letters, just published by Smith, Elder & Co., Thackeray speaks of Horace Smith (who has been once or twice mentioned in these pages) in the following eulogistical terms:—(Could a finer panegyric be uttered over any man's grave, or a grander epitaph be inscribed on his tomb-stone?) "That good, serene old man who went out of this world in charity with all in it," and proceeds to associate him with those who possess "the precious natural quality of love which is awarded to some lucky minds, such as Charles Lamb, and one or two more in our trade."

The following poems refer to the Almanack on page 21, and were published about the same time :—

> " Quid dignum tanto feret hic promissor hiatu?"—*Hor.*
>
> This is a line I learnt some time at School,
> It signifies "Great cry, and little wool."

Personal, pointless, without rhythm or wit
Your Almanack has failed to make a "hit."
To form it three calves' heads in one were roll'd,
No wonder the amalgam yields no gold!
The triple brains, a compound mass of mud,
Have not produced a single line that's good.
Nothing to glad the eye, nor shake the side—
With such a subject, and a field so wide!
For keen bright sarcasm, we have instead
Blunt impudence, that aims not at the HEAD.
The great triumvirate expires in trash ;
The lengthened labour brings forth—balderdash.
But oh, "proh pudor!" was there not a man
Amongst the tuneful trio that could scan?
Walk in, ye men of satire, look around,
Here, butts for every skilful shaft abound :
See characters of every mould and hue ;
Humbugs and false men side by side with true.
Look not for cripples, nor the halt or blind—
Few here are faultless both in form and mind.
Lo ! a buffoon, a fool, a spendthrift, glutton,
A millionaire, or miser—like poor *Mutton*.
Here's servile meanness, cringing wealth before ;
And avarice that toils to grasp at more ;
Conceit with learning ; modest worth *without* it :—
'Tis here you'll find them all, sirs, never doubt it.
Behold extravagance, assumption, pride,
And honest poverty, and worth well tried !
Lads too, who lavish all upon their dress,
Nor yet disguise their native snobbishness.
Since here, then, neither men nor matter lack,
We look for *something* in your Almanack.
Though short the *measure*, yet there's quite enough
In that sixpenn'orth of inferior stuff :
And none had grumbled, had there been still less on't,
For shades of "*Smith*," "*Hook*," "*Hood*," you've made a
    mess on't !

If Punch be sold for three-pence, then by jingo,
Six-pence is dear for such poor limping lingo!
When next your hands you try at it—if ever—
Poetic junta, give us something clever.
   A *name in type* beyond these walls may pass,
And clubs and *salons* write you down an ass.
So as an axiom take it, or a hint—
Scurrility should never be in print.
Or else some morning, ere the man has lunched,
The *Publisher* may get his pipkin punched.
'Twere vain to try the Author's brains to scatter,
Those heads, alas! can boast not even batter.
From throes Parnassian, such a tiny mouse
Will add but little *lustre* to the "house,"
From whose high dome, yon bright and starry crown
(If managers would let it) would come down!
Not round your brows a wreath of light to twine,
But on the darkness that's within to shine.
The chance was good, and the materials glorious;
The failure is complete—the *fact* notorious!

G. L.

Dehinc, ut quiescant porro moneo, et desinant
Maledicere : malefacta ne noscant sua.

Which means pray be quiet and shun broken bones,
Those who live in glass houses should never throw stones.

    There was an aged poet once
      Who bought an Almanack,
    And on that periodical
      Composed a fierce attack.

    For he, as page by page he read,
      More cross began to look,
    To find the couplets he composed
      Omitted from the book.

    The fact was, that the publisher
      Had made a little fuss;
    And would not print old Fogie's jokes,
      They were so libellous.

    The kindest heart resents neglect,
      Revenge, a passion worse is;
    But wicked was the pride that set
      Our poet making verses.

In grand hexameters he wrote,
  A heavy coach for wit;
For who would take a ten-inch gun
  To shoot at a tom tit?

With harsh abuse his lines began,
  To fisticuffs alluded;
Cracked a few feeble jokes, and then
  With more abuse concluded.

They came out on a Saturday,
  And on the Monday morn,
Full many a member came to town,
  With visage woe-begone.

If any friend the reason asked,
  Thus answered was his question;
That poem's disagreed with me,
  And brought on indigestion.
                                P. S.

RUNNING A BULL.

VERSE ON A BROKEN-DOWN MERCHANT, 1695.

" Trampling the Bourse's marble twice a day,
Though little coin thy purseless pockets line,
  Yet with great company thou art taken up,
For often with Duke Humphrey dost thou dine,
  And often with Sir Thomas Gresham sup."

PARI PASSU (PEAR I PASS YOU)
HALF DIS TO PAR.

SONGS.

THE BULL MOVEMENT.
BY A BEAR.
Air—" By-and-by."

Gambling will be all the go,
   By-and-by.
Tapes you'll find in every show,
   By-and-by.
Blondin on the tape will walk,
Writing with a piece of chalk
Opening prices from New York,
   By-and-by.

Wabash Pref. will go to par.,
   By-and-by.
Atlantic First much higher far,
   By-and-by.
And you'll not be able to
Buy for cash whate'er you do,
Invert Sugar or Peru,
   By-and-by.

Ebbw Vale at fifty-five,
   By-and-by.
Such a corner we'll contrive,
   By-and-by.
Rio Tinto shares will be
Thought quite cheap at sixty-three;
And we'll all so happy be,
   By-and-by.

When the top at last is gained,
   By-and-by.
Bulls all rampant unrestrained,
   By-and-by.
Suddenly will supervene
Quite another sort of scene;
You will find out what I mean,
   By-and-by.

HOUSE SCRAPS.

The following refers to "The Callao Bis," which was brought out some years ago:—

"THE CALLAO BIS."

Air—"The Mistletoe Bough."

A minstrel sat down to write a line,
The theme of his verse was the Callao Mine;
The finest mine in the world was this,
And the name of this mine was the Callao Bis.
          Oh, the Callao Bis, &c.

They found a nugget of such a size,
They said the prices were sure to rise;
Eleven thousand pounds it weighed,
And bets about it were freely laid.
          It came from the Callao Bis, &c.

It wasn't the mine call'd the Callao Old,
Of which, I dare say, you've oft been told,
A better by far than that, was this,
So they called it—The Callao Bis!
          Oh, the Callao Bis, &c.

It found its way to Parisian halls;
The Frenchmen scrambled to pay the calls;
And the demi-monde and the heavy swells,
And the men on the Bourse with their howls and yells.
          Oh, the Callao Bis, &c.

The farmers sold their sheep and swine,
To buy the shares of the Callao Mine.
The finest mine in the world was this,
And they called this mine the Callao Bis.
          Oh, the Callao Bis, &c.

But the market "beared" them all the same,
For they saw from the first the little game,
Which was much of the sort, as the syren's kiss,
Played to the tune of the Callao Bis.
          Oh, the Callao Bis, &c.

And still the market are bears, are bears,
And nobody sees any rise in the shares;
And the price is now about one to the three,
With another pound liabilitee.
          Oh, the Callao Bis, &c.

THE POWER OF LOVE.

When Balfe's "Satanella" was produced at the Lyceum, in 1858, one of the melodies ("The Power of Love") became very popular, almost everybody hummed or whistled the air; the street organs disturbed quiet neighbourhoods by grinding it out upon the slightest provocation. One afternoon it was sung to a newly-engaged member, amidst great enthusiasm, other love-sick members were hunted down and also "baked," dozens of jokers insisting upon shaking hands and congratulating the lucky one, who had to run the gauntlet of a lot of chaff. What took place, for a joke, that afternoon, almost at once became a custom of the House, and has continued so to the present.

RECIT.

Myself once more, the page I cease to play;
All woman now, my soul resumes her sway;
Tho' conscious love his wakeful heart denies,
In dreamful visions let me charm his eyes!
One blissful moment in my true form seen;
By love enthroned, his fancy's worshipp'd Queen!

CAVATINA.

There's a pow'r whose sway
    Angel souls adore,
And the lost obey,
    Weeping evermore;
Doubtful mortals prize
    Smiles from it above,
Bliss that never dies,
    Such thy pow'r, oh love!
Source of joy and woe,
    Foiler of stern hate,
Lord of high and low,
    Woman calls thee Fate;
Fierceness owns thy spell,
    Vulture thou, and dove,
Language cannot tell
    Half thy pow'r, oh love.

Song, sung to a jobber in the Unified market, 1884 :—

Air—"Tiddy-fol-lol."

He's got ten thousand a year,
    Tid-dy fol lol, Tid-dy fol lol,
And his view is always clear,
    Tid-dy fol lol, Tid-dy fol lol,
On the rise or on the fall,
With the brokers great and small,
He is the don of all,
    Tid-dy fol lol, tid-dy fol lol, etc.

Song, as sung to jobber in Russian market, 1886 :—

Air—" Father, dear father, come home with me now."

O, Edmund, dear Edmund, come back to me now,
The markets continue to drop ;
You promised, dear Edmund, to keep up the price,
And now I'm left in at the top.
I'm an awful big bull of Peru and Domain,
Of Daira and Unified, too ;
Just try if you can't puff the market again.
"Yes, Pa ! I'll see what I can do."

Song, as sung to a jobber in Egypt market, 1884 :—

Air—" The Empty Cradle."

Trying hard a decent income to secure,
   In the Egypt market day by day;
How can I make money? business is so poor;
   But now that Pat is absent I can play.

Play from morn to eve, boys, eleven o'clock till four,
   Cutting a few losses on the way;
Leaving Barclay Greenhill grilling at the door
   To keep the pot a boiling while I play.

Brother's left the market when he jobbed before,
   Leaving me and Barclay here all day,
Gone with Dale and Fletcher, peace for ever more,
   Now that Pat is absent I can play.

Tho' the song's a good one and will make you roar,
   Keep it dark until another day;
Pat might cut up rusty and begin to jaw,
   You'd better sing the song when he's away.

Tune—"The Wooing o't."

When Major P—— has his lunch,
    Bang goes a bawbee, O!
He has an oatmeal cake to scrunch,
    Bang goes a bawbee, O!
Major P——'s unco' sly,
There is no green about his eye,
And O! it makes the Major cry,
    When bang goes a bawbee, O!

When the London Scottish meet,
    Bang goes a bawbee, O!
When the Major stands a treat,
    Bang goes a bawbee, O!
But O! the day is unco' rare,
For siller he has nought to spare,
And O! it makes the Major swear,
    When bang goes a bawbee, O!

When a body posts a sonnet,
    Bang goes a bawbee, O!
He puts a postie stamp upon it,
    Bang goes a bawbee, O!
But O! the Major's unco' wise,
To save his cash he always tries,
And postie cards he always buys
    And saves half his bawbees, O!

[The above was sung to a jobber in the Unified market, 1883.]

The following lines were sometimes sung to one or two well-known members :—

    "La-di-da, La-di-do,
    He's a well-known old Adonis,
    La-di-da, La-di-do,
    You may tell it by his nose,
    La-di-da, La-di-do,
    For the colour all his own is,
    'Tis a pleasing combination
    Of the beetroot and the rose."

Popular song, frequently sung to a jobber in the Foreign market, 1886 :—

Air—"The Ghost of Christopher Binns."

I'm the ghost of John, James, Christopher, Benjamin Mills,
Left this world cut off in the midst of its mischief and ills;
My home is down below, I'm only here for an hour or so,
For when the cocks begin to crow, good-bye, Benjamin Mills.

LIGHT THE DIPS, THE SAINT IS COMING.

Song, sung to Mr. C——:—

    Air—" The Vicar of Bray."

    In bad Queen Mary's bloody reign
        The land was full of tortures,
    She racked the Protestants with pain,
        See Foxe's book of Martyrs.

    But good Queen Bess, of glorious name,
        The true religion nourished;
    Great Briton earned a deathless fame
        And Protestantism flourished.
Oh! why don't you read, don't you read, don't you read,
        Oh! why don't you read?
            Foxe's Book of Martyrs.

Another song, sung to the much-persecuted Mr. C——:—

    " Hymn Tune."

    Light the Dips,
    The Saint is coming,
        Swing the incense round,
    See the gorgeous devil-dodgers
        Bowing to the ground.
    Hark! my soul, the bell is tinkling,
        Lo! St. Chittles smiles,
    Priests in stained-glass attitudes
        Are crawling round the aisles.
    Swing the Pots,
    St. Chittles cometh,
        Send the relics round,
    Kiss the dirty skull and relics
        Dug up from the ground.

On several occasions all the clocks in the House stopped or went wrong; this generally happened when Mr. R. Bristowe (Manager) was away. In August, 1886, the following was posted in the House:—

    Air—" Grandfather's Clock."

    Mr. Manager Bristowe gave us a clock
        Which we look at in wonder and awe,
    And he planted its face in a circular space
        Cut in marble above the front door.
    But with sorrow we learn that through " waiting for a turn,"
        Its credit with time has run down;
    For it's stopped short, and can't go " tick " again
        Till Bob's back in Town.

The following song was sung to a popular jobber, 1884:—

Tune from "Orpheé aux Enfers."

When the market's rather heavy,
And the brokers in a bevy
Crowd around me, I endeavour to sell them stock so dear;
Ha! Ha! Ha!
Ho! Ho! Ho!
Jolly go the moments when I rook them so.
Ha! Ha! Ha!
Ho! Ho! Ho!
Jolly go the moments when I rook them so.

But I sometimes get a smarter,
When I buy stock at a quarter,
And I find that demon Slaughter is banging far below.
Ha! Ha! Ha!
Ho! Ho! Ho!
What a wretched trade it is when things are so.
Ha! Ha! Ha!
Ho! Ho! Ho!
What a wretched trade it is when things are so.

The following (a parody on the popular song [1884] "In the Gloaming," by Lady Hill) was often sung to a firm of jobbers in the Trunk market, about 1884:—

"Things are gloomy, Oh! my Dorling,
Let us sell a Trunk or two;
Prices round us all are falling,
It were best for me and you.
Though my voice is hoarse with puffing,
Lower prices still we'll see;
It were best to sell them, Dorling—
One for you and *two* for me.

Song, sung to popular jobber in Unified market, 1883:—

Air—" Three Jolly Sailor Boys."

A brave old sportsman lives in Romford town,
    And Walker seems his name to be.
At jobbing he's won great renown,
    But at playing who is half so good as he.
How funny when the market's making money—
That it's tip, tip, tip,
    Off go the hats so free;
But he sees us in his glasses,
And he calls us all Jackasses
    When we try to catch him on the H. O. P.

The following is a parody on a popular song "Old Clo! Old Clo!" (1886), and was often sung to a jobber in the Unified market, during 1886.

"Old Clo! Old Clo!
Any old hats, I buy 'em,
And when your coats are rusty brown
Just take them round to Hyam.
    I prowl about the House,
    But I find it is no go,
I'm going to give up Unified,
And buy Old Clo!"

To the air of "Another Row Downstairs."

Now Mr. P—— and Chuncky C——
Wore flowers for a lark,
    And insulted old P—— unawares;
But old P—— came and caught 'em,
And before the beaks he brought 'em,
    For another jolly row downstairs.

Now we think it is a pity
That our ever-wise committee
    Should encourage men to give themselves such airs,
For they think we cannot match 'em,
But in March we mean to scratch 'em,
    Or there'll be another row downstairs.

The following was frequently sung to a member during 1885 and '86:—

   Air—" Ting! Ting! that's how the Bell goes."

" Mi-ow, Mi-ow ! "—that's how the cat went,
" Mi-ow, Mi-ow ! "—crying below ;
  Under the bed,
  Hiding her head,
Poor little Pussy went " Mi-ow, Mi-ow, Mi-ow ! "

Joe, Joe ! fly to the rescue ;
Joe, Joe, in his night shirt flew,
  Poking his nose
  Under the clothes,
To find where poor Pussy went " Mi-ow, Mi-ow, Mi-ow ! "

Joe, Joe ! now we must ask you ;
Joe, Joe ! please let us know :
  After the sport,
  When Pussy was caught,
Why did the Pussy go " Mi-ow, Mi-ow, Mi-ow ? "

One verse from a parody on " Far, Far Away ! " Sung to a popular member:—

  There is a lodging-house
   Not far away,
  Where they have onion soup
   Three times a day.
  Oh ! how those lodgers yell
  When they hear the dinner bell ;
  And how their bellies swell,
   Three times a day.

The following was sung to a popular family about 1883:

  Tune—" We are a Merry Family,
    We are ! we are ! we are ! "

Jack, he deals in Canadas,
  In Trunks, one, two, or three ;
Willie, he gives turns away,
  But not to *you* or *me;*
The young 'un goes to music-halls,
  And does the la-di-da ;
We are a shiney family,
  We are ! we are ! we are !

Chanted to an old member, about 1880.

> Boko's nose is strong,
> Boko's nose is long;
>   'Twould be no disgrace
>   To Boko's face
> If Boko's nose were gone.

A Pre-Raphaelite Portrait—My Loeb! My Love!

The following was sung to a popular jobber in the Foreign market a few years ago:—

Air—"Willie, we have Missed You."

> Oh! Alfred, is it you dear?
>   Safe here once more;
> Our hearts have been with you, dear,
>   On Sicily's lone shore.
> But here you are again,
>   And it makes our hearts rejoice,
> To hear you cry, "here, Puckle,"
>   In that well-remembered voice,
> "Take in stock at six per cent.,"
>   When the rate is only four.
> Oh! Alfred, we have missed you,
>   Welcome home once more.

The following was sung to a most respected member about 1881:—

Air—"In the Coming Bye-and-Bye."—From "Patience."

> "Slender once I used to be,
> All the girls did look at me,
> Each one wishing she might be,
> Chosen bride of R. J. C.
> Corpulent I have become,
> And these boys they think it fun
> To call me the aldermun
> > Of the coming bye-and-bye.
>
> But when I become Lord Mayor,
> Let these naughty boys beware;
> Turtle soup they shall not share,
> Bread and water shall be their fare.
> I'll give them in custodie,
> They shall taste Q.U.O.D.,
> If they dare to sing to me,
> > In the coming bye-and-bye.

The following parody on "Far, far away!" was sung a few times in the Old House during 1885.—From Christmas Number of *Truth*, 1884.

I.

> "Where is our last big *coup?*
> > Far, far away!
> Where are our profits too?
> > Far, far away!
> Till in our indigence
> We think of getting hence,
> P'raps clients have less sense,
> > Far, far away! Far away! Far away!

II.

> Where are those specs we made?
> > Far, far away!
> Where is our quiet trade?
> > Far, far away!
> Once we had mansions fine,
> Now lodgings are our line,
> In two pair backs we pine,
> > Far, far away! Far away! Far away!

III.

Gone are our prancing steeds,
  Far, far away!
Gone those expensive weeds,
  Far, far away!
Gone with our mashing suits,
Gone with our varnished boots,
Gone with our hot-house fruits,
  Far, far away! Far away! Far away!

IV.

Once there were bogus lines,
  Far, far away!
Likewise much salted mines,
  Far, far away!
Oh! how we bulled the shares,
Then how we turned to bears;
None now such sells prepares,
  Far, far away! Far away! Far away!

V.

P''raps folks can still be done,
  Far, far away!
So we will cut and run,
  Far, far away!
Here swindles now are vain,
But once across the main,
We may pick up again,
  Far, far away! Far away! Far away!

Sung to Mr. C——, to the air "I am such an Artless Thing."

When first I dealt in stocks and shares,
  It was astonishing;
  I am an artless thing!
  I am an artless thing!
They always took me unawares,
  Being an artless thing;
  When up come the brokers—
  Those artful old brokers—
Those leary old jo-o-o-o-kers.
  "Oh! Mr. C——, tell me,
   What are Defence, and B. and C.?"
    "The market is doubtful,
     I'll just go and see,
   For I am such an artless thing."

THE LOST GATE.

NOT BY ADELAIDE A. PROCTOR.

[THE ARGUMENT.—Mr. Yesmar, after dozing blissfully one eventide, awaketh to find his garden-gate missing. He bemoaneth his fate, and indulgeth in a denunciation of the midnight marauder, who, he appeareth to think, is one named Arabi Nospmis.]

  Seated one night in my parlour,
   I was happy and had no fears,
  And my fingers wandered lightly
   Over the cup that cheers.

  I was feeling rather sleepy,
   For the hour was growing late,
  When I heard a dreadful creaking,
   Like the noise of my garden-gate.

  It rose o'er the fumes of 'baccy
   In that frosty air so still,
  And seemed to my troubled spirit
   Like a foretaste of coming ill.

  It stirred up my bilious liver,
   Like the edge of a rasping knife,
  And raised a discordant echo
   Of a misspent bachelor life.

  It rent all my blissful dozings,
   It banished my dreams of peace,
  And trembled away into silence,
   As if it were loth to cease.

  I have sought, but I seek it vainly,
   That garden-gate so fine,
  Which vanished from off its hinges,
   Whilst I dozed o'er my barley wine.

  It may be that Arabi Nospmis
   Of his exploit now is vain;
  It may be that wily sinner
   Will be up to his tricks again.

  It may be he'll grow more reckless
   If no notice now is ta'en;
  But I'll set the law in motion,
   If he collars my gate again.

ANOTHER SONG ON THE SAME SUBJECT.

Air—"Oh where! Oh where! is my Little Wee Dog?"

Oh where! oh where! is my garden gate,
Oh where! oh where! can it be?
    In the dead of the night
    Some villanous wight
Ran off with my G. A. T. E.

While I sat at the club, which we hold in a Pub,
I boozed till I couldn't well see,
    But I'm ready to swear
    That the gate was still there,
Tho' I couldn't quite manage the key.

When I rose in the morn
I found it was gone,
For the gardeners told it to me;
    I made up my mind,
    Tho' perhaps 'twas unkind,
'Twas done by that thief Arabi.

Alas! poor Oliver, I knew him well.

A popular member caught a tame hen-pheasant, which he put in a coop and proceeded to fatten for some festive occasion. This coming to the ears of some jocular members, a bogus telegram was sent to his wife saying, "Shall bring Walker to dinner; prepare pheasant." The pheasant was killed and eaten *en famille*. The following song was sung to the member next day:—

ST. CHITTLES AND YE PHEASANT.

Air—"Who killed Cock-Robin?"

"Who killed the pheasant?"
"I," said Chittles,
"I wanted some victuals,
I killed the pheasant!"
    All the brokers and the jobbers
    Are sighing at present,
For they've heard of the death of the poor hen-pheasant.

"Who saw it die?"
"I," said Tom Qui,
"With my little eye,
I saw it die!"
    All the brokers and the jobbers,
        etc., etc.

"Who caught the blood?"
"I," said Brooks,
"When it went off the hooks,
I caught the blood."
    All the brokers and the jobbers,
        etc., etc.

"Who'll eat the bird?"
"I," said Walker,
"Tho' I didn't stalk her,
I'll eat the bird."
    All the brokers and the jobbers,
        etc., etc.

The following verse was sung some few years ago to—nobody in particular:—

Tune—"Three Blind Mice."

Three German Jews,
See how they run;
They all run up and down Angel Court,
Saying, "Preference and Unified ought to be bought,
For the 'bull' account isn't as big as you thought."
Three German Jews!

HOUSE SCRAPS.

The following song was only sung once to a firm of jobbers in the Foreign market. The occasion being when they started an agency in Paris (1884).

Air—"Over the Garden Wall."

We're going to job on the Boulevards,
   Over the other side;
We've even issued our business cards,
   Over the other side;
We're going to do without Spenser, called Tom,
And Hagan to us will in future belong;
We're pulling the strings both hard and strong,
   Over the other side.

CHORUS.

Oh! over the other side,
   The profits we'll divide;
The venture is young, but we won't be done
Our fortunes to make we've only begun;
What a fine double-book we'll be able to run,
   Over the other side.

Sung to T—— Q——, October 25th, 1887:—

Air—"The Vicar of Bray."

In days gone by, when Peru were eight,
   I offered many a score, sir,
And vow'd we'd not have long to wait
   Ere they would be but four, sir.
And now I sell as I did then,
   They're on the downward caper,
"Give five away!" Yes! Yes! they say,
   E'en tho' they are waste paper.

CHORUS.

So if your luck you'd like to try,
   And *the* right thing would do, sir,
Just take the advice of Tommy Qui,
   And sell a few Peru, sir.

Last week a tip they set afloat,
   That over fifteen topped 'em,
But Rothschild's welcome little note
   Soon back to fourteen flopped 'em.
For I am out beyond a doubt,
   And so they may go hang, sir;
If you're out too 'tis well for you—
   Let's both go in and "bang," sir.
      Chorus as before.

THE FATE OF "GORGONZOLA HALL."

We could at last no longer fight against our crushing fate,
So "Gorgonzola Hall" got turned into "New Billingsgate."
Whilst we, deprived of pears and nuts, and "sweeties" bought of "Dunny,"
Went out into the world to try to make a little money.

Some of us turned photographers, the lords regained Mayfair;
"Stephen" into the wine-trade went; and "Bob," in his despair,
Took to the road with tracts; whilst "Jack and Harry," reft of hopes,
To active training went, forthwith, inside the stakes and ropes.

"Laurence and Pat" became M.P.'s; and, when he was not preaching,
"Jack Long" was little Bible tales to Sunday scholars teaching;
"Bennie" to Mormon Land returned; and "Little Ted" at last,
Across St. George's Channel to his bog-girt mansion past.

"The Major" in his Highland home, upon his bag-pipe wailed;
"Richard" his little lonely barque across th' Atlantic sailed;
"The General's" wild laugh thenceforth at Aldershot was heard;
"The Colonel's" sternly martial tones the Shorncliffe echoes stirred.

"Peabody" "dashed his wig," and ceased to hunger for "more books;"
"Algy" no longer brushed his hair, regardless of his looks;
"The Lion's" roar was checked at last, and even "Joe" grew thin;
And "John" went to his old port wine and much-loved violin.

HOUSE SCRAPS. 175

To Sanger's "Little Gus" repaired, to play a super tar;
"Arthur's" melodious shrieks in "Trunks" no more were heard afar;
"The Skipper" he a-hunting went, whilst "Lacy's" ceaseless zeal
Made him upon the cinder-path the "Demon of the Wheel."

And now at night the Huntsman Wild the Yankee market sees,
Amongst blue lights and murmurs of in-nu-mer-a-ble Bees!
But never now, 'midst soft "miaows" is "Poor Old Joe!" discerned,
Nor is the "Saint" asked solemnly if he his bread has earned.

"The Chevalier" his organ and his monkey both regained;
But "Edmund" in its place no more his eye-glass dull maintained.
The "Grasshopper" was silent, too; "King Cole" no jokes advanced;
His Majesty the "King of Spain" no "Options" now financed.

The "Captain" his much-swelling chest in breastplate did install,
And then went off to do his best to ornament Guildhall.
In short, all hied this way or that, at Fate's so harsh decree,
Till Capel Court was empty as the mull of "W. B.!"

Truth, Christmas Number, December 25th, 1884.

Sung to B—— G——, 1887:—

Air—"The British Grenadiers."

Some talk of Major Puckle,
   And some of Toney Pearse,
Or else of General Richardson,
   So warlike and so fierce.
But of all the valiant soldier-men,
   The ladies' hearts to kill,
There's none compare for military air
   With Barclay C. Greenhill.

We wouldn't give pain to Cecil Fane,
   Or even Grenville Grey,
Who've worn their brilliant uniforms
   On many a bloodless day.
But spite of all their bravery,
   Our hearts with joy do fill,
When we gaze with pride on the martial stride
   Of Barclay C. Greenhill.

BULLS AND BEARS.

Sung at the Dinner for the Benefit of the Fund
FOR
DECAYED MEMBERS OF THE STOCK EXCHANGE,
5th JUNE, 1844.

Of a song you have the *Call*, and I *Put* it to your votes, sirs,
If this *Call's* not worth as many *Pounds* as I give singing *Notes*, sirs,
Since here we've met to raise a Fund, by Charity induced, sirs,
To aid Decaying Members whose *Consols* are all *Reduced*, sirs.
  " Bulls" and " Bears," cease all animosity and drown your cares.

In Speculation's troubled sea 'tis difficult to float, sirs,
And many sink by cramming all they have into one boat, sirs,
Some reach a sorry *Terminus* who deal in *Iron Railings;*
Men may forgive our faults, but they can't forget our *Failings*.
  " Bulls" and " Bears," &c.

Misfortunes seldom come alone, but then a *Loan* is wanted,
Yet having no *Securities* a *Loan* is never granted,
The *Bonds* we've held in them we find taste more of gall than *Honey*,
Our dealings are *"done for the account"* and we are *dunn'd* for money.
  " Bulls" and " Bears," &c.

From these *Chili Bonds* of poverty our Brothers to release, sirs,
Our *Active* aid we'll not *Defer* their comforts to increase, sirs,
For we possess within ourselves, by a happy combination,
The Elemental principles that form a wealthy nation.
  " Bulls" and " Bears," &c.

A *King* we have among us, though a *Tudor* does not reign, sirs,
He has a *Chamberlain*, a *Knight*, and a *Burgess* in his train, sirs,
Our *Cannon's* always ready, should an enemy attack us,
We've *Major*, *Man*, and *Moore*, disposed with friendly views to *Backus*.
  " Bulls" and " Bears," &c.

We're rich in *Fields*, have sunny *Hills*, some *Greenhills* it is true, sirs,
Our *Vignes* and *Flowers* (I do not *Bragg*) are flourishing to view, sirs,
Our *Barnes* are stored with *Pepper-Corne*, our *Woods* are full of game, sirs.
Our *Brooks* and *Waters* teem with fish, and we've *Worms* to catch the
    same, sirs.
  " Bulls" and " Bears," &c.

Our State is very tolerant in its religious views, sirs:
Our *Abbot* wears his surplice, we don't persecute the Jews, sirs;
We've *Parsons*, *Clarks*, and *Chaplins*, too, of all *Sex*, down to *Shakers;*
We in *Abbey* and in *Chappell*, *Chant*, and likewise *Foster Quakers*.
" Bulls" and " Bears," &c.

Free trade is our principle, we have no secret lurkings;
If you do not like our *Brewer*, why there's *Barclay* and there's *Perkins;*
Our *Taylors*, *Coopers*, *Bakers*, *Barbers*, all of profits boasting,
But our *Goldsmids* are the people who really make the most Tin.
" Bulls" and " Bears," &c.

Our Gardens Zoological in wonders do abound, sirs,
And a perfect happy family in them is to be found, sirs:
Our *Lyons* never growl and fight and snarl about a *Bone*, sirs,
Our *Wolfe* is never *Badger'd*, but enjoys his lamb alone, sirs.
" Bulls" and " Bears," &c.

Now the greatest curiosity amongst our birds you'll find, sirs—
Though a talking *Starling* is not rare, nor a *Martin Swift* as wind, sirs—
But we defy the world at large, in any other house, sirs,
To catch a singing *Peacock!* why it beats the singing mouse, sirs.
" Bulls" and " Bears," &c.

My *Carroll's* nearly ended, but in this large community
We should not pass the *Short*, the *Small*, the *Little*, with impunity,
For every little *Helps* to swell the fund of which we boast, sirs,
So " Success to it, and health to all," shall be my general toast, sirs.
" Bulls" and " Bears," &c.

To this toast I'll add a sentiment, and then conclude my lay, sirs,
Though rather contradictory is what I have to say, sirs,
May you long support this noble Fund, and generously employ it,
But I *Hope* I do not see one here who ever will enjoy it.
" Bulls" and " Bears," &c.

HARRY TOMKINS.

Jack and Gus on the Warpath.

Bull Dog and Pup.

HOUSE SCRAPS. 179

Jack and Gus ashore.

Mr. Godwin.

180 HOUSE SCRAPS.

STOCK EXCHANGE PUZZLE; "Find the Small of Joe's Back."

Wm. Bristowe fecit.

HOUSE SCRAPS.

SUBSCRIBERS TO THIS WORK.

Limited to 200.

A.
Adams, J. S.
Albert, F. M.
Allen, W. P.
Allen, A. E.
Angle, J. B.
Ashby, F. W.
Atchley, W. W.
Atkin, E. T.
Atkin, H. W.
Aubrey, H. J.

B.
Bacchus, R. F.
Baker, L. J.
Baker, L. Ingham
Barry, jun., H.
Bellars, W. B.
Birks, H. W.
Borrow, H.
Bouverie, Hon. K. P.
Bower, G. C.
Boyer, F. H.
Braggiotti, H.
Bristowe, T. L. (M.P.)
Bristowe, Wm.
Brown, M. M.
Brunton, H.
Bryant, E.
Burge, J.
Burge, W. A.
Burgess, J. J.
Butterworth, A. H.

C.
Caldecott, J. B.
Campion, Fritz
Carlisle, C. H.
Carr, Wm.
Cawston, Geo.
Chamberlain, Wm.
Chappell, S.
Chapman, J.
Christie, Alex. H.
Christopherson, S.
Chaldecott, A.
Clarke, W. P.
Colliver, Fred.
Combe, J.
Concanon, J. B.
Cohen, Leo L.
Cohen, Frank
Coulson, H. W.
Cork, A. C.
Crocker, Alf.
Crosdale, Alf.

D.
Da Costa, E.
Daly, J.
Daw, J.
Dawson, C. F.
De Boos, W. L.
Dickinson, K.
Docking, W. C.
Dyall, F.
Dyall, A. A.

E.
Ellissen, G.
Erskine, L. R.

F.
Francis, J. S. D.
Freene, A. M.
Freeman, Frank
Fletcher, C.

G.
Gould, F. C.
Gilling, J. F.
Gledstanes, F. G.
Grant, J. S.
Gray, Geo.

H.
Hadrill, W. F.
Hartridge, W.
Hartridge, C.
Harris, H. B.
Haes, H.
Heathcote, J. A.
Herbert, S.
Helyar, F. W.
Homan, L.
Homan, R.
Hobday, F. M.
Hodge, L. F.
Hoghton, C. A.
Holl, E.
Hollebone, C.
Hodgson, J.
Hurst, P.

HOUSE SCRAPS. 183

I.
Ingram, Geo.

J.
Jacks, jun., A.
Jackson, C. H.

K.
Kalker, S. M.
Kellaart, E. F.
Kennedy, S. E.
Kindell, A. A.
Kitchin, T. M.
Kitchin, Geo.

L.
Lawrence, E. H.
Lefébure, Albert E.
Levien, F.
Lewinger, C.
Livermore, F.
Lobb, A. F.
Lucas-Calcraft, J.

M.
Maguire, S. C
Martin, J.
Mares, R.
Mason, W. H.
Meyer, Hartwig
Milbank, F. H.
Miéville, L. C.
Midlane, H.
Morris, C. A.
Morris, W. J.
Moore, Wm. Turle
Mullens, J. A.
Montefiore, A. Sebag

N.
Neall, J. W.
Neall, W. P.
Nickalls, C
Nickalls, P.
Nivison, R.
Nye, T.

O.
Odell, F.
Oliver, T.
Oliver, H. St. John

P.
Palmer, Alf.
Parker, J. W.
Petre, Hon. A. H.
Phillips, A. J.
Phillips, Layton
Phillips, W. J.
Price, C.
Price, W. J.
Puxon, E. W.

R.
Ramsay, R.
Ramsay, J. J.
Ray, Herbert
Read, J. F. H.
Regensburg, A. L.
Reidpath, T.
Reynolds, A. L.
Ridsdale, E. A.
Robertson, J.
Robinson, F.
Roden, Geo.
Roehrick, E.
Rooff, P. H.
Roughton, A. H.

S.
Schmidt, B. J.
Scott, Hamilton
Scott, S. W.
Scrimgeour, W.
Simmons, Ed.
Simon, H. I.
Skinner, J.
Sly, A. H.
Smith, Edmund
Spenser, J. D.
Speyer, Arthur
Spurling, P.
Staples, H.

Stein, C.
Surgey, C.
Surgey, T.
Sutherland, H.

T.
Tagg, J.
Taylor, F. G.
Terry, T.
Thomas, D.
Thomson, D. L.
Tilleard, F. D
Topham, J.

V.
Vallance, A. H.
Vandervell, W. F.
Van-Raalte, C.
Vaughan, J. H.
Vertue, Alf.

W.
Walker, J. S.
Walker, W.
Ward, J, B.
Ware, R. E.
Wearne, H.
Wetenhall, H. H.
Wetenhall, J. G.
White, C. A.
Whiteheads, J.
Whittington, C. J.
Wildy, L.
Wilkinson, A. W.
Wilkinson, C.
Wilkinson, D.
Wilkinson, H.
Wilkinson, Tarral
Williams, Owen
Wilson, T. H.
Woodroffe, F. H.
Wornum, R.

Y.
Young, A.

Z.
Zanchi, V. B. M.

LONDON:
PRINTED BY CHARLES AND EDWIN LAYTON,
56, FARRINGDON STREET, E.C.

UNIVERSITY OF CALIFORNIA LIBRARY
Los Angeles
This book is DUE on the last date stamped below.

PR
1195 Atkin -
S8A8 House scraps

PR
1195
S8A8

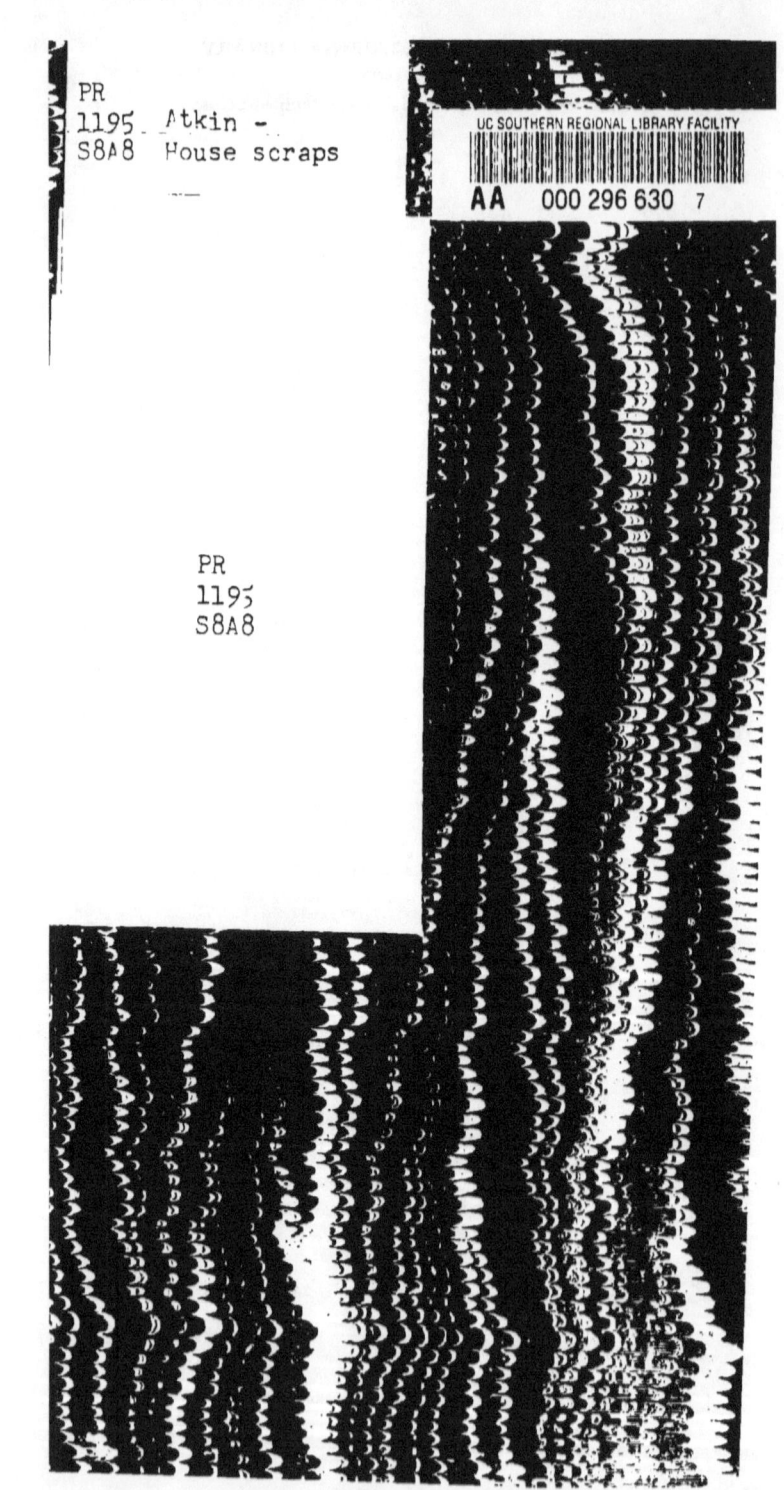

www.ingramcontent.com/pod-product-compliance
Lightning Source LLC
Chambersburg PA
CBHW022018220426
43663CB00007B/1126